The Power of Learning

Andrew Mayo and Elizabeth Lank were colleagues at ICL at the time of writing, a European information technology company that operates across the world and enjoys a leading HR reputation.

Andrew Mayo is now a consultant and lecturer, specialising in helping organisations manage learning and development more effectively. He spent nearly 30 years in industry, the last 10 in a senior international HR role at ICL. A graduate in both Chemical Engineering and Management Science, he worked for Procter and Gamble in several posts before taking up personnel, marketing, and general management positions in various other companies. In recent years he has written numerous articles and chapters in books, including one on 'Economic indicators of HRM' in *Strategic Prospects for HRM* (edited by Shaun Tyson, IPD, 1995). His first full-length book, *Managing Careers*, was published by the (then) IPM in 1991. He is a Fellow of the IPD.

Elizabeth Lank is responsible for knowledge management at ICL, a post that arises out of her work on learning organisations. A graduate of Mount Holyoke College in Massachusetts and the INSEAD MBA programme, she has had an international career in the information technology industry. She joined ICL in 1986, where her previous roles have all been concerned with leadership and management development, with a strong focus on the link between learning and business performance.

Other titles in the series:

Changing Culture: New organisational approaches
Alan Williams, Paul Dobson and Mike Walters

The Communicating Organisation
Michael Blakstad and Aldwyn Cooper

Empowering Change: The role of people management
Christopher Ridgeway and Brian Wallace

Ethical Leadership
Stephen Connock and Ted Johns

From Leanness to Fitness: Developing corporate muscle
Michel Syrett and Jean Lammiman

HR Effectiveness
Jim Matthewman

Leadership for Strategic Change
Christopher Ridgeway and Brian Wallace

Management Development: Strategies for action
Alan Mumford

Managing Careers: Strategies for organisations
Andrew Mayo

Managing the Mosaic: Diversity in action
Rajvinder Kandola and Johanna Fullerton

The Reality of Strategic HRM
Michael Armstrong and Phil Long

View from the Bridge
Geoff Armstrong

The Institute of Personnel and Development is the leading publisher of books and reports for personnel and training professionals and students and for all those concerned with the effective management and development of people at work. For full details of all our titles please telephone the Publishing Department on 0181 263 3387.

The Power of Learning

A guide to gaining competitive advantage

Andrew Mayo

and

Elizabeth Lank

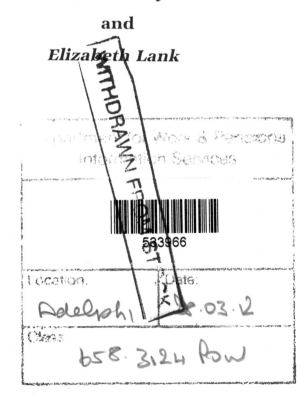

THE INSTITUTE OF PERSONNEL AND DEVELOPMENT

First published in 1994
Reprinted 1996, 1997

Typeset by Photoprint, Torquay
Printed in Great Britain by
The Cromwell Press, Wilts

British Library Cataloguing in Publication Data

*A catalogue record for this book is available from the
British Library*

ISBN 0–85292–565–4

The views expressed in this book are the authors' own, and may
not necessarily reflect those of the IPD.

INSTITUTE OF PERSONNEL
AND DEVELOPMENT

IPD House, Camp Road, London SW19 4UX
Tel: 0181 971 9000   Fax: 0181 263 3333
Registered office as above. Registered Charity No. 1038333
A company limited by guarantee. Registered in England No. 2931892

Contents

Acknowledgements

Writing this book has made us very conscious of how much more we have to learn about learning! There have been many thinkers who have, over the years, shaped our current understanding. Networks such as the European Foundation for Management Development have broadened our perspectives and contacts considerably. We owe a great deal to our colleagues at ICL for the stimulating environment of experience, experimentation and sharing which they provide.

We are especially grateful to David Megginson of the Sheffield Business School, Alden Lank at IMD, Alan Mumford, and our colleagues Peter Kennedy and Norman Pickavance for their helpful comments on our manuscript, to which we hope we have done some justice.

Last but not least, our gratitude goes to Elisabeth and Keith, who have not only coped with much more at home than should be reasonably expected, but who also contributed from their own experience to the development of our thinking.

Preface

'People in this company never learn!' So said the 53-year-old who saw for the nth time people making the same mistakes he had seen made 20 years before. Is it inevitable that every organisational generation must learn the same things over again for themselves?

The term 'Learning Organisation' has achieved increasing attention since the late 1980s and received a significant boost with the publication of Peter Senge's milestone work '*The Fifth Discipline*' in 1990. Is it but a set of new clothes for dressing up old ideas? Or is the assertion from the Book of Ecclesiastes that 'there is nothing new under the sun' a caution just to get on with business and avoid another fashionable diversion? And if there is some value to the ideas, how can they be translated into something practical against which organisations can be *measured*?

We are convinced that the essence of survival and competitive advantage for organisations is to be found in the reality of the Learning Organisation. The *label* used to describe it is less important than the understanding of the notion itself: namely that *survival* in a rapidly changing world is dependent on *adaptability*; adaptability is dependent on the *capability to learn*; and that capability is dependent on the *motivation* for continuous learning of everybody in an organisation within a *supportive learning environment*.

In fact, every activity is a potential source of learning; every success and failure, each customer comment, all are examined within organisations *to a greater or lesser degree*. We would argue that learning is more than the acquisition of knowledge, however: it is acquiring information or knowledge and doing something *differently* as a result. We believe that the difference between those who treat learning as an *accident* and those who treat learning as a *deliberate business process* is the difference between those who will eventually fail and those who will succeed.

In this book we are not so interested in the precise definition of terms or the development of conceptual models. Our aim is to provide a means of *benchmarking* your organisation against the characteristics of a mature Learning Organisation. If your organisation is only 20 per cent of the way towards the ideal, and your competitors are at 40 or 50 per cent, then you are certain to be at a competitive disadvantage.

We have used the notion of *power* as a theme. This is because a lot of what happens in organisations is about power in one way or another, an aspect that some academic writers don't always recognise. It also has the connotation of strength and energy, and that is how learning needs to be perceived in organisations – as a vital force to be given attention and investment in every aspect of the organisation's life.

We offer as our definition of a Learning Organisation the following:

> A Learning Organisation harnesses the full brainpower, knowledge and experience available to it, in order to evolve continually for the benefit of all its stakeholders.

We also suggest that the business-based learning organisation can be broken down into nine linked elements, as illustrated in the model of The Complete Learning Organisation which appears on page 235. This shows that creating business value is the end goal of learning, but that the effectiveness of learning is fundamentally dependent on the learning environment. We examine the enablers of a supportive culture in Chapters 1 to 4:

- policy and strategy resulting from the conviction that *managing* learning is the essence of success
- leadership
- people management processes
- information technology.

We examine aspects of the culture itself in Chapter 5. The next three chapters look at effective learning at the personal, team, and organisational levels. Finally, we consider how all these elements link together to create value.

After each section we ask a number of questions under the heading *Powerpoints* to enable you to benchmark your organisation – recognising that the answers will rarely be black or white but will be on a spectrum that takes account of:

- whether the *means* are in place
- the extent to which the means are *utilised*
- the extent to which the means apply to *all parts* of the organisation being measured.

The *Powerpoints* are brought together in the Appendix to form the basis for a Learning Organisation Index (see pages 237–62).

To create a true Learning Organisation is particularly challenging in large, complex organisations but we believe the principles apply to large and small, complex and simple. Whether you are the leader of an organisation, an individual working within one or a professional human resource development specialist, we hope that you will find the chapters that follow both thought-provoking and of immediate practical use. If they help you to develop ways of increasing the effectiveness of your organisation, then we will have achieved what we set out to achieve.

Andrew Mayo and Elizabeth Lank

1

The Power of Learning as the Essence of Success

The pressures of change

In the 1990s a real awareness of the fundamental truth that organisations are only as good as their people has finally emerged. What company chairmen write as a matter of routine – that 'nothing could have been achieved without the excellent efforts of our employees' – has ceased to be lip-service and become a vital truth. In his 1993 Annual Report CEO Jorma Ollila of the Finnish Nokia Group devotes some 70 per cent of his summary to issues of people and values – a refreshing change from the traditional discussion of achievements 'despite difficult trading conditions'. This truth is not just about people working hard, but about the *capability* and *skills* of everyone contributing to the organisation. It is also about the organisation itself as an entity and the way in which it utilises the competence available to it, and adapts to meet the challenge of its environment in ways that are distinct from its competitors.

It always seems that the pace of change has never been greater, and indeed it is easy to show on a variety of parameters that the rate of change *is* accelerating through the years. Planning horizons become shorter, skills become out of date quickly, expectations on quality and service reach ever higher levels, and organisations that have enjoyed a reputation for excellence for years can suddenly find themselves on their knees. Charles Handy calls it 'never-ending whitewater', a picture of foaming turbulent currents. The greatest external influences on organisations today are economic, and more and more organisations are subject to global market forces whether they like it or not. Technology and deregulation are two of the forces driving massive change – causing global product commodities, alliances of all kinds, changing competitive balances, and forcing cost out of businesses in uncomfortable

1

ways. The need to be faster to market, with *international* products and services, at competitive cost, quality and delivery levels is causing unprecedented pressure.

These forces change the barriers to entry for new competitors. Such new entrants do not bring the 'baggage of history' in bureaucracy, overheads, established workforces and entrenched cultures that the older companies have. They have immediate cost advantages – and thus put pressure on all suppliers in the sector. The trend to deregulation also upsets established monopolies and creates new forms of competition. *Whether on the attack or on the defence, the winners are those who learn fast and who mobilise most effectively the combined learning of all contributors.* These contributors embrace the broadest possible range of intelligence, innovation and experience available. There is no doubt that this speed of learning is harder for the well-established organisations than it is for the newcomers.

It is this challenge that is driving organisational transformation, causing traditional models of hierarchy and structure to be questioned. Such forces are unlikely to go into reverse. We are not talking about fashions here, but fundamental questioning of many comforts that we have taken for granted over recent decades. Reg Revans first coined the formula many years ago that:

$$L >= C$$

That is, the pace of learning in organisations and individuals must equal or be greater than the rate of change being faced. This is a fundamental law of survival. In these turbulent times, with change happening so fast, the need to *manage* learning in the organisation rather than leave it to chance is even more pressing. Most educational suppliers offer events in the management of change; how many in the corresponding management of learning?

The task is not to be the best *predictor* of the future but to be more *responsive* to change than our competitors. To quote John Kay, a professor at the London Business School:

> The decline of IBM was not the result of a declining demand for computers, and Pan Am did not go bust because people stopped flying. The failure of these companies followed not from the disappearance of their markets, but from their inability to see or respond to the changes taking place within them.

The average life of the large industrial enterprise is about 40 years, roughly half the lifetime of a human being. Most organisations are not good learners, despite their high-flying statements of intent. The larger and more bureaucratic they are, the less easy it is to be so. But organisations have very little choice - 'adapt or die' are the stark alternatives that face them.

We might well ask: 'Is not learning a natural process? If we get good people, encourage them to get the training they need, will not the "Learning Organisation" take care of itself? In the end isn't it just a question of good management, giving people opportunities, keeping up with the competition – doing what we've always done?'

Of course learning *is* happening all the time. People are assimilating new information, learning from mistakes, having good ideas and implementing them every day. Pockets of excellence are to be found through individual efforts and capability in nearly every organisation, just as pockets of excellent customer service are found. But many opportunities are being lost every day because there is no *systematic* understanding of what enormous potential is available. To create a complex culture that is *characteristically* a Learning Organisation requires a dedicated and co-ordinated framework which creates the appropriate language, the appropriate processes, the supporting systems, the commitment and involvement by *every* individual, and – consequently – which leads to the achievement of success for that organisation.

Learning Organisations – what do they look like?

Many have attempted to define and describe a Learning
Organisation, and also the learning process both for individuals and organisations. Indeed, many of the recent changes
in thinking have been associated with the latter. The teaching-
led approach has been strongly challenged by a self-managed,
person-centred approach to learning, and debate continues as
to whether individual learning effectiveness can be transferred
effectively for the benefit of the organisation. As Bill Critchley
observes in the AMED Focus paper on the subject, 'many of
the ideas are not new at all . . . organisation development
practitioners in the 1960's and 1970's espoused systematic,
empowering principles as well as the key goal of helping
organisations learn how to learn'.

But there is a new reality of the economics of survival for all
organisations which is leading them to realise the importance
of effective learning. This happily coincides with a different
way of valuing people in an organisation. The Learning
Organisation is frequently associated with this as well as new
approaches to organisational structure. Charles Handy describes
his own vision as follows:

> Such organisations will continue to defy conventional
> wisdom. They will be organisations of consent, not control.
> They will be able to maintain a feeling of togetherness
> despite their size and farflung locations. They will make
> many mistakes, but will have learned from them before
> others realise they occurred. They will invest hugely and
> save the salaries of ranks of inspectors. Above all they will
> see learning not as a confession of ignorance but as the
> only way to live. It has been said that people who stop
> learning stop living. This is also true of organisations.

He sees learning as a continuously rotating wheel of four
quadrants – questions-ideas-tests and reflections. This process
lies at the heart of individual growth and corporate success.
Keeping the wheel moving requires the five concepts of:

- *subsidiarity* – giving away power, defining the boundaries of jobs, and placing decisions at the most appropriate level
- *clubs and congresses* – opportunities for people to meet and greet
- *horizontal fast tracks* – variety of assignments to give continuous learning
- *self-enlightenment* – individual responsibility for learning
- *incidental learning* – learning from the happenings of the everyday life.

Handy is a visionary, but many of his concepts and models make so much sense that we observe organisations deliberately working to them as a way forward.

Many ideals and models for learning have been put forward in the literature. Some are essentially behavioural, others focus on a supportive learning climate for individuals, and are closely linked to cultures of empowerment and individual ownership. Professor Chris Argyris of Harvard has become well known for his distinction between 'single loop' and 'double loop' learning. The former is about the correction of errors within a defined system; the latter the questioning of the system itself. Double loop learning involves re-examination of the fundamentals, which may lead to *unlearning* previously held views of the world. Such fundamentals might be, for example, the way organisations are structured, the role of individuals in them, or the way performance is monitored.

Ikujiro Nonaka in a much-quoted 1991 article in the *Harvard Business Review* entitled 'The knowledge-creating company' asserts that the sole business of an organisation is innovation. He uses Japanese learning practices to illustrate his belief that 'knowledge is the capacity for "effective action" – the emphasis is on "know-*how*" rather than "know-*what*"'. Thus going away on courses, especially outside the organisation, would be generally regarded as a strange form of learning compared to that to be obtained from doing things. Nonaka contrasts the 'objective processing' of information that characterises Western thinking with the Japanese subjective and shared insights. There the collective commitment to an identity and purpose

immediately puts new knowledge in the shared domain, so that
its enhancement becomes iterative and mutual. So an individual's
learning is naturally transferred to become organisational
knowledge.

Some feel the need to rethink our concepts of learning, to be
more aligned with the Japanese approach. This seems to us to
be unhelpful, since we are dealing with individuals and organisations with deeply different sets of values, ingrained from an
early age. We may envy the ease of knowledge transfer that
Japanese organisations achieve, and look for ways to emulate
it in a Western way, *but* we have to find ways which build from
our own cultural heritage.

The term 'Learning Organisation' as a specific description
dates from books by Bob Garratt of the UK (1987, 1990) and
Peter Senge of the Sloan School of Management, MIT (1990).
In one of the best-known books on the subject, Senge outlines
five 'disciplines' of the Learning Organisation:

- *personal mastery* – continuous learning by the individual
- *mental models* – examining the ways in which we view the
  world
- *building a shared vision* – something that pulls everyone
  towards a common long-term goal
- *team learning* – thinking together and producing results
  better than the members would on their own
- *systems thinking* – seeing the relationships between all the
  components of the organisation.

For Senge, the last one is the key. He calls it 'The Fifth
Discipline', that holds the others together and necessitates the
completely new way in which individuals see themselves and
their world. His definition of a Learning Organisation is 'one
that is continually expanding its capacity to create its future'.

Many have attempted their own descriptions of the components of the ideal Learning Organisation in recent years. We
have found particularly helpful Swieringa and Wierdsma's
book *Becoming a Learning Organisation*, and Burgoyne,

Pedler and Boydell's continuing work with the Learning Company Project. The latter lead a movement in sharing ideas and experiences in learning itself.

Starting with the business perspective

There is a strong focus on culture and behaviour in many of the models proposed. There is no doubt that the attention given to learning and a supportive learning climate over the last few years is a step forward, both for individuals and organisations. Much of the work that has been done is really helpful to practitioners. More recently, attention has increased in the area of the transformation of the structure and processes of organisations, driven by pressures of change as outlined earlier. Economic and social forces are putting a new onus on individual responsibility for continuous learning.

Yet there is a need for a *business-centred holistic approach* that looks first at what positively *enables* continuous learning for individuals and the organisations in which they work, and then second that relates learning to benefits in terms of *measures of success*. These measures include:

- return on assets
- image and brand
- customer satisfaction
- reputation as an employer
- successful alliances

- market share growth
- productivity increase
- innovation
- survival and growth
- employee morale.

We repeat from the Preface our suggested definition of a Learning Organisation as the following:

A Learning Organisation harnesses the full brainpower, knowledge and experience available to it, in order to evolve continually for the benefit of all its stakeholders.

Such an organisation succeeds by ensuring that a range of *inputs* are available, such as surveys, competitive data, performance measures, ideas and suggestions, benchmarking data, market research, and the learning from daily experience; that the *processes* of listening, analysis and synthesis, feedback, information storage, dissemination, access, and sharing are effective – *leading to* learning at all levels and thereby improved measures of success.

Each organisation should look at its own needs, both current and as derived from its objectives for the future, and describe the characteristics it would like to aim for in order to be a competitive Learning Organisation. Some of the References may help here (see pages 263–5) in parallel with the approach we have taken ourselves.

 POWERPOINT

Does your organisation have a template describing the characteristics of the kind of Learning Organisation it would like to be?

Does your organisation have a framework and a plan for practical implementation to achieve the desired state?

Why this is vitally important to the stakeholders

We should understand before proceeding any further what the *business benefits* of an integrated total approach to learning will be. Many organisations still base their success exclusively on bottom-line financial measures. However, the work of Robert Kaplan and David Norton in explaining the concept of the 'balanced score-card' recognises that financial results are the *result* of achieving success on a range of measures. This approach links performance measures in four areas:

- How do customers perceive us? (customer perspective)
- What must we excel at? (internal perspective)

- Can we continue to improve and create value? (innovation and learning perspective)
- How do we look to shareholders? (financial perspective)

Goals and measures can be defined under each of these headings. In a second article the authors describe how various companies have applied and adapted this approach as a strategic measurement system.

Following on from this principle of balance, organisations have different sets of *stakeholders*. We will look at the benefits to the three that are core to all – customers, employees and shareholders.

Benefits for *customers* include:

- *making available to customers products and services that meet their evolving requirements more effectively than competitors'*. If we want to maintain customer loyalty and attract new ones we need to be capable of removing any motivation to go to competitor suppliers. Keeping ahead necessitates superior knowledge, skills and attitudes among our people and being able to utilise those in the organisation speedily and effectively for customer benefit. Some organisations have created *partnerships* with customers to enable mutual learning from each other, and from third parties.
- *the rate of innovation, not just in products or services, but in process adaptability and responsiveness*. The pace of change today requires a corresponding pace of innovation. This has traditionally been looked for in products, but more and more we see it in services and in the effectiveness of internal processes. This innovative approach has to be throughout the organisation – 'reinventing the corporation', as the business process re-engineers would call it. So the systems and processes, the entire culture and the 'space' that people have in which to use their initiative, need to change in innovative ways for customer benefit.

 **POWERPOINT**

Does your organisation compare with the best competitors in innovation for customer benefit?

Does your organisation regularly survey customer perceptions of responsiveness to their needs?

Where feasible, does your organisation encourage partnerships with customers for mutual learning?

Benefits for *employees* include:

- *the ability to enhance both internal and external employability*. A Learning Organisation encourages all individuals to take a personal stake in their continuous learning within a supportive and encouraging environment. Each employee plans and replans improvements in their portfolio of knowledge, skills, attitudes and experience – to be able to meet the challenges of the present and the future, either within or without a particular organisation.
- *the opportunity for better job security*. Security can never be guaranteed in today's organisations in terms of jobs for life, or even for any period of time. Some will not be able to keep their personal learning at the pace needed. But an effective Learning Organisation achieves sustained success in achieving its objectives and provides the best possible opportunities by creating new roles to meet new customer demands.
- *a sense of self-respect*. The Learning Organisation is one that values individuals and their contribution irrespective of any hierarchical position. It is one of open communication, where people are not afraid to take risks or make some mistakes. It is flexible, and not bound by rules and procedures except where they make good business sense. It is a rewarding place to work, where helping each other is a normal part of continuous learning.

 **POWERPOINT**

Do employees respond positively through opinion surveys or other methods of upward feedback about their perceptions of learning processes and how they help them?

Would your organisation be regarded as a 'preferred employer'?

When people voluntarily leave the organisation is it rare to give reasons such as lack of growth opportunities?

Benefits for *shareholders* include:

- *differentiated human assets that have more value than those of the competition because of their capability*. Talented people are the most precious asset. People are attracted to an organisation that shows it can develop and motivate its people. A Learning Organisation is one that not only has a reputation for its focus on learning but is constantly improving the processes it has for developing the potential of all its people.
- *minimising voluntary losses of good people*. The most common reason for people wanting to leave organisations voluntarily is the lack of challenge in their work, and of forward opportunities. This should not happen in a Learning Organisation, which understands why it *needs* to give people continuing challenges, and therefore learning opportunities.
- *the reduction in layers of management and functional controlling staff as people take more responsibility themselves*. De-layering is made possible as we re-examine and change the roles of the different levels, and is a very substantial cost-saving in organisations. Individuals and teams are given freedom to fulfil their roles without the need for levels of supervision and direction in their tasks.
- *the reduction of costs as continuous improvement yields continuous productivity increase*. An organisation that is

continually questioning itself and looking for better ways to achieve its objectives will be one that shows resulting productivity increases, as it eliminates waste and is continually searching for lower-cost methods.

- *the elimination of duplication and overlapping activity as the parts of the organisation share and learn from each other, rather than competing internally.* This is probably the greatest area of invisible cost in an organisation – the unwillingness and inability to learn from others in it. Those ignored may be predecessors, colleagues or sister-units in the organisation. Devolution and empowerment can reinforce this tendency, even though we will argue strongly for the learning benefits that they can bring. But the costs here are enormous. Every reorganisation, change of team members or loss of key individuals brings losses in productivity as new learning is needed. So often this learning happens in isolation, on an individual basis, rather than through a comprehensive plan.

  The costs are not just in inefficient learning by individuals. It can be the case that whole projects are unnecessary as problems are solved that have already been solved elsewhere. Or research may be commissioned that has already been done before. These are easily measurable and avoidable bottom-line costs.

  A Learning Organisation has the capability of remembering and making available to all its members its collective knowledge and experience. Moreover it has a culture that assumes it is normal to access such knowledge before embarking on new ventures, and that means respecting the work of others. It is a strange phenomenon that people often find it much easier to talk with, and respect the work of, others who are outside the organisation rather than inside it!

- *the ability to seize market opportunities through speed of adaptation and change.* Learning capability is not just about making sure that the organisation's current business can survive. It is also about looking for the new. When everything appears to be operating against you, and you are focusing on cost-cutting and downsizing it is sometimes difficult to focus instead on looking beyond the problems for the new opportunities. The effective Learning Organisation does that constantly, evaluating new possibilities.

- *the availability of the right people with the right skills in the right place at the right time.* The winning organisation today is the one that has the right skills available at the right time to be able to seize business opportunities of all kinds. The investment in continuous learning is essential to this end. Companies like Andersen Consulting spend around 7 per cent of fee income annually to ensure their people are continually up to date and adding greater value to their stock of human capital. They see it not as a cost, but as an investment.

 POWERPOINT

Is your organisation structured in a way that encourages freedom and risk-taking, and minimises low added-value layers of management?

Can your organisation show continuous productivity improvement for all its groups of employees?

Does your organisation look for and quantify costs arising from unnecessary duplication and overlap?

Are the skills and capabilities of your people such that they are sought after by other organisations?

Strategy and core competence

Having considered the importance to the stakeholders of the Learning Organisation, we should consider at this stage the strategic planning process. An organisation cannot plan ahead effectively without giving careful thought and analysis to the capabilities it will need to meet its objectives and strategies. Every financial, product, marketing or service strategy has implications for organisational and human resource capability.

If there is no plan to realise them, it is highly unlikely other strategies will succeed.

In doing strategic planning we look at our chosen markets or service sectors and decide where we would like to be positioned in them, in the context of the overall organisation, its mission and aims. We modify those endpoints in consideration of the environment in which we operate. This may mean taking account of political, economic, competitive and government influences. Once we have a view of the endpoints and the main strategies, we begin to look at how they may be achieved. We need to study the changes needed in the organisation or parts of it in terms of:

- *structure* – geography, global:local, matrix, lines of business, vertical or horizontal, resource centres, mergers, alliances, JVs
- *culture* – values, norms, rewards
- *capability* – resource numbers and mix, roles, knowledge, skills, attitudes and experience, processes, systems.

There is the risk of assuming that the capability needs will solve themselves, so long as we get the 'headcount' right. 'Headcount' as a control has become an anachronism, as organisations look at their resources more flexibly, particularly service providers. The Learning Organisation recognises that individuals have different values, and that some contributions will come from 'core' employees and others from 'peripheral' suppliers. What matters is first, the total cost of supply of human resources and second, the decision as to what skills will be in the 'core'.

Indeed Prahalad and Hamel, in their articles in the *Harvard Business Review*, would argue that the strategic planning process should start with an understanding of the 'core competences' of the organisation and work forward from there. In a study by management consultancy McKinsey's on high-performance organisations, they chose 'world-class competencies' as one of the six parameters. Prahalad emphasises that core technologies should not be confused with core competence. He defines a core competence as something that:

- is a significant source of competitive differentiation
- transcends a single business
- is hard for competitors to imitate

It can be conceptualised as:

Competence =

(technology × governance process × collective learning)

By 'governance' Prahalad means the way the organisation works together; by 'collective learning', the creation of a learning environment at all levels. He concludes that technological predominance can be subservient to the other two factors, and this has been amply demonstrated by the struggle of powerful technological companies like IBM in the early 1990s.

Organisations do well to evaluate their core competencies as a critical component of their strategic planning.

 **POWERPOINT**

Has your organisation evaluated systematically its core competencies and are they used in strategic planning?

Does your organisation evaluate all strategic plans in terms of its human capability to deliver?

A positive policy and strategy

The Learning Organisation brings benefits to all. In particular it is essential for survival in a turbulent world. Senior management needs to be explicit about this in the articulation of their policies and strategies.

When the Rover Group in the UK were identifying key strategies as part of their total quality programme, one of the nine they came up with was 'continuous learning'. They defined this as:

the process by which the business identifies, acquires, disseminates, retains, shares and updates useful knowledge.

The development and organisation of this process was made highly visible by creating the 'Rover Learning Business'. The primary aim of this 'business within a business' is to provide a top-quality learning and development service to all employees. Its first chairman was Sir Graham Day, at that time chairman of the Rover Group itself. In addition to the encouragement of personal learning, it established a corporate learning database capturing key learning points from all business activities. Amongst many achievements, they would cite the establishment of 'learning' on everyone's agenda as the most significant. Their critical success factors are summarised as:

- *creating a culture* that provides purpose, dignity and recognition to every individual in an environment of trust which is open, safe and secure
- *helping the leaders to lead* by empowering and supporting them in pursuit of company goals
- *achieving world-class resourcing standards* – ensuring they have the right people in the right numbers with the right skills, in the right place at the right time
- *creating continuous learning* with development opportunities for everyone and sharing of best practice
- *ensuring company-wide understanding of the compelling business needs* by maintaining continuous dialogue
- *empowering individuals and teams* to achieve success through commitment, motivation, flexibility and skills development
- *fostering positive involvement relationships* with the broader Rover community.

Sir John Harvey Jones said in 1992 that, 'If there was an award for the most changed company I would give it to Rover'. We feel their approach is certainly a role model.

POWERPOINT

Does your organisation have a defined policy statement that specifically supports the development of a Learning Organisation?

Does it communicate clearly to all employees the ways in which it will encourage and enhance such development?

Pointers for action

The pressures of change being experienced by every organisation today necessitate continuous learning and adaptation in order to survive. Life is ever more complex; the amount of information available is incredibly large and rapidly increasing. The real competitive advantage of organisations is their ability to use the information available to them, and the capabilities of all their people to provide better products and services for their customers.

All organisations are Learning Organisations in the sense that *some* learning cannot be avoided. What separates the weak from the strong is the ability to increase, harness and manage the learning for the benefit of the whole organisation. The characteristics that bring success are complex and strike to the heart of historical cultures, structures and processes. The reality is that the organisation that harnesses the power of individual learning through teams to the benefit of the whole entity brings advantages to all its stakeholders, and ensures its growth and survival.

The recognition of this should result in explicit policies and strategies – which are communicated clearly to all. There are different ways in which this might be done. Some actions that can be taken are:

- ensuring explicit statements are made about continuous learning, benchmarking, and knowledge-sharing in statements of direction and strategy

- appointing a senior experienced person to manage progress towards being a better Learning Organisation
- featuring specific endgoals relating to being a Learning Organisation in organisation-wide communications, especially those from the chief executive or equivalent
- ensuring that guidelines for budgeting state the expectations of levels of investment in learning
- ensuring that the values of the organisation reflect learning as an essential investment that must be shared.

Finally, an organisation should ensure it understands where its core competence lies, and how it builds on it in developing its strategies.

2

The Power of Leadership

From managers to leaders

With the incredible pressures on organisations today, it is little wonder that leaders in these organisations are finding themselves under tremendous pressure too. The demands on management capability come from many sources:

- cost-cutting initiatives that reduce resource levels
- flattening organisational structures that shorten communication links but increase so-called 'spans of control'
- complexity and volume of information to be absorbed
- the need to manage complex webs of joint ventures and alliances with suppliers, customers, and competitors
- devolution of accountability from HQ/central functions to business units
- the need constantly to invest in skills updating.

In the midst of this confusion one thing is clear – for a successful leader in today's world, the established set of managerial competencies will not suffice. The things managers have been taught for decades are meant for a different, more predictable, more orderly world. Traditional management tools and techniques are aimed at organising resources to create successful results in a relatively stable world. Forecasting, budgeting, organising, monitoring, reviewing: this is the langauge of the task-centred manager. These traditional skills are still essential to make things happen but a much broader capability is required from the people occupying leadership roles today.

The dictionary definition of 'manageable' is 'easily made subservient to one's views or designs'. Not surprisingly, many previously successful managers are feeling distinctly uncomfortable. As they reach for the management tools in their kitbag, they find that some have become obsolete and that the kit is incomplete – in a chaotic world, things are no longer so 'easily made subservient'. The leadership skills previously considered the province of CEOs are now required in many different roles at all levels in the organisation.

In *The Transformational Leader* Tichy and Devanna highlight the difference between a 'transformational leader' and a 'transactional manager'. A transformational leader can inspire people to make quantum leaps into the unknown while a transactional manager makes tangible, measureable things happen. We need far more transformational leaders in today's turbulent world, in businesses that require radical transformation and renewal rather than maintenance management. In a June 1994 *Financial Times* article discussing the remarkable comeback of the IT company Unisys, Alan Cane quotes a colleague of CEO James Unruh describing his boss as one who 'sees the butterfly the caterpillar can become, not an improved caterpillar'. As organisations devolve accountability to their component parts, this kind of visionary thinking is not the role of the few but of the many.

In an April 1988 *Harvard Business Review* article, Shell's planning director, Arie de Geus, who helped to develop the concept of 'scenario planning' at Shell, said that 'the ability to learn faster than your competitors may be the only sustainable competitive advantage'. The challenge is to identify the people who will be able to transform our organisations into these learning engines and lead them into the 21st century.

Take me to your leader

The distribution of leadership is more widespread in Learning Organisations – there are the 'official' leaders at the top of the old-fashioned boxes of the organisation chart; the charismatic individuals throughout the organisation to whom people turn for inspiration; the temporary heads of project teams and task forces who lead for a time and then step back into their individual contributor roles; the individuals who set up special interest groups and networks, and take them forward. In his book *Leadership is an Art*, Max De Pree of the successful furniture company Herman Miller called it 'roving leadership' – 'the ability of hierarchical leaders to permit others to share ownership of problems'. Far more roles in our organisations call at least occasionally on some leadership capability.

The Learning Organisation moves away from the notion of an élite stream called 'management', vested with their own special status, to a much wider sharing of leadership skills across the organisation. Power is distributed; the person at the helm of the ship still has a vital role to play but control processes are replaced with shared accountability. It is this accountability that encourages initiative, experimentation, risk-taking, and learning.

 **POWERPOINT**

Does your organisation provide the opportunity to develop leadership skills to anyone with a requirement for those skills, regardless of hierarchical position?

A picture of a leader

There have been many studies of this new emphasis on leadership, each taking a slightly different perspective. In *A Force for Change* John Kotter said: 'Leadership produces change. That is its primary function.' Peter Senge put it as follows in *The Fifth Discipline*: 'leaders are designers, stewards, and teachers . . . that is, they are responsible for learning'. With the requirement for more leaders in more places across organisations, the qualities required to lead successful Learning Organisations need to be well understood and well communicated.

From our own observations, we would suggest that there are six essential qualities for leaders in a nimble, continuously learning organisation, at any level.

A leader in a Learning Organisation is a:

- visionary
- risk-taker
- empowerer
- learner
- coach
- collaborator.

Whereas in the past leaders were expected to be heroes who 'led from the front' and gave the orders, the new attributes give much more of a sense of *leading from within*, as part of a team rather than remote from it. We will look at each of these attributes in turn to consider what they mean in practice.

Visionary

With the uncertainty and ambiguity that surround us, leaders must have the creative and intuitive ability to draw a mental picture of the organisation they wish to create, giving people in the organisation an aiming point, the lighthouse beacon in the storm. Particularly in today's difficult world of cost-cutting and other pressures, there needs to be a positive focus for the energies of the people who survive the waves of redundancies. Gary Hamel uses the term 'strategic intent' to describe the direction set by leaders – the word 'intent' implying a certain flexibility along the way. With the changes around us, an agreed target is essential but the way to it is likely to become clear over time.

Leaders must shape their vision and be able to communicate this vision to others in such a way that the ownership of that vision is shared across the organisation. Peter Senge considers 'shared vision' to be one of the key characteristics of a Learning Organisation:

> a shared vision . . . provides a rudder to keep the learning
> process on course when stresses develop . . . With a
> shared vision, we are more likely to expose our ways of
> thinking, give up deeply held views, and recognize
> personal and organisational shortcomings.

A shared goal lifts people above the petty diversions that can otherwise become a focus. Athletes reviewing team performance are open about their own mistakes and genuinely wish to improve for the sake of winning the next game. Musicians rehearse and learn from their errors, aiming to achieve the best possible result on the night of the performance. Without a shared goal, the fallback position is 'looking out for number one' – far more defensive behaviour and unwillingness to be open to learning is the frequent result. For a sports team or a symphony orchestra, individuals with different personal agendas can be disastrous. Though less obviously so, they can also be catastrophic for a business organisation.

A vision must be shared rather than simply imposed on others. Leaders need to create participative processes which give people at all levels in the organisation an opportunity to contribute to the thinking that shapes the future of the organisation. Time needs to be invested in open sessions that enable a vision to be discussed, understood and refined with a wide group of stakeholders. At Deutsche Aerospace (DASA) a process of strategic dialogues was created at which board members regularly discuss their vision for DASA with a wide group of DASA managers and employees. This gives people the reflection time needed to understand what that vision means to them and the opportunity to share their views and thoughts on the way forward, hence accepting some ownership of the company vision for themselves. Some companies are now investing in facilities for satellite television broadcasts that enable company leaders to communicate world-wide – with the possibility of audience participation.

A shared vision is a powerful motivator: if individuals are inspired to reach that shared goal, they will overcome many obstacles in order to do so. Komatsu's 'KILL CATERPILLAR' focus or Fujitsu's 'BEAT IBM' were examples of communicating a clear strategic intent, relative to *competitors*. The highly successful Swedish furniture retailer Ikea has the vision of improving the quality of everyone's everyday life through low-cost, well-designed furniture – a motivating, *customer-focused* vision. A shared vision leads to *quantum leaps* in performance rather than mere incrementalism. A shared vision generates *passion and commitment* and helps individuals to cope with the pain of change along the way.

 POWERPOINT

Do leaders in your organisation have a clear and shared vision of where the organisation is heading?

Is their vision developed over time with the input of many members of the organisation, at all levels?

Is their vision communicated effectively to all within their sphere of influence, using two-way communication processes?

Risk-taker

Today's leaders must be prepared to take risks. The world we live in is unpredictable and in some cases decisions must be taken which are largely a leap of faith. For example, ICL chose to spearhead a move towards open systems in the computer industry – freeing customers from the restrictions of one manufacturer's proprietary systems – at a time when this went completely against conventional wisdom. That courageous decision is credited as a major factor in the company's subsequent success. Leaders must have the courage to risk their personal reputations on a few well-chosen big bets. They need even greater courage and strength of character to accept that not every big bet will pay off – and to share publicly the lessons learned when that happens.

Leaders must also create environments in which risk-taking is encouraged. Leaders can take calculated risks in many ways:

- developing people by putting them into stretching roles
- devolving financial authority to low levels
- throwing away the rule books
- investing in innovation
- testing new market opportunities
- creating alliances with competitors
- encouraging experiments and prototypes.

Motorola describes one of the necessary mindset shifts for their managers as moving from a 'know-and-do' attitude to a 'practice-and-experiment' outlook. Without experimentation and risk, there is unlikely to be much innovation or creativity.

In *Lateral Thinking for Management* Edward De Bono has pointed out the need for a new language to free managers from their reluctance even to suggest new, innovative and risky ideas. If you introduce a proposal by saying, 'I think we should consider doing this . . .', you inextricably link yourself with the idea – and your self-esteem with the acceptance of it. De Bono coined the word 'po' to use as a signal that what you are putting forward is a provisional idea, one that may not be perfect but is worth exploring. By saying 'this is just a "po"' before introducing the idea, your self-esteem is protected if the idea is explored and then rejected by others. Leaders can make it safe to put forward a 'po' by encouragement and example.

With uncertainty and unpredictability a way of life, risk management is a critical skill for today's leaders. Whether success or failure results from a risk taken, the learning benefit is likely to be of high value. The only unpardonable sin is that of failing and then *not learning* from it.

⚡ POWERPOINT

Do your leaders take calculated risks?

Do they learn from mistakes and share that learning with others?

Do they encourage creative dialogue and the putting forward of innovative, risky ideas?

Do they encourage experimentation?

Learner

A leader's response to risk-taking highlights the importance of his or her being a personal role model for learning. It is impossible to create an environment for others in which learning is a key focus if the people in leadership positions seem to be saying that learning is a case of 'do as I say, not as I do'. The symptoms of this disease are relatively easy to spot at an organisational level:

- an absence of management development activities at senior levels in the hierarchy
- little or no contact between senior managers and anyone other than their direct reports
- no processes for making continuous improvement suggestions or weeding out difficulties/problems from within the organisation
- few benchmarking activities
- little customer contact at senior management levels.

In *Learning to Lead*, Bob Garratt writes:

> It is rarely acknowledged that once a person is promoted to the direction-giving level of an organization, they will need any development at all . . . What a major paradox there is here – that at the time people make their biggest career change from a specialist job to general management, and have the biggest impact on their organization if they don't perform well, they are given the least support!

Leaders, particularly at top levels, must take responsibility for their own learning and development. Role model behaviour is relatively *easy* to spot and would include the following:

- Keep a personal development plan and communicate its contents.
- Seek and utilise personal feedback and counselling.
- Welcome and encourage challenges to the status quo, and suggestions for continuous improvement.

- Foster a wide range of contacts – employees at different levels, customers, competitors, best-practice benchmarks.
- Review learning points from situations that don't go as planned. This often means creating institutionalised learning processes such as:
  - an embedded process for reviewing why something went wrong eg why a particular sale wasn't won – and for considering how to prevent this from occurring in the future; (an example of such a process might be as simple as a 'Learning Points' agenda item at the end of every regular management meeting)
  - a process for turning feedback from customer satisfaction surveys into remedial actions
  - a process for reviewing and communicating the output from employee opinion surveys and taking action on the concerns.
- Admit personal mistakes and share the lessons learned.

Leaders must create processes to ensure that learning is reinforced and shared. Above all in this, they must set a *personal* example.

⚡ POWERPOINT

Do leaders in your organisation set the example by consistently reviewing and sharing learning points from different experiences?

Do they welcome challenges to the status quo?

Do leaders in your organisation each have a personal development plan?

Empowerer

'Empowerment' of employees, combined with the elimination of double-checking and monitoring/controlling functions, is sometimes perceived as a risky business. Managers who are used to being the decision makers and approvers feel somewhat out of control. In his book *Liberation Management* Tom Peters describes it as:

> . . . an extraordinary paradox. You are out of control when you are 'in control'. You are in control when you are 'out of control'. The executive who 'knows everything', who is surrounded by layers of staffers and inundated with thousands of pages of analyses from below, is 'in control' – just like those central planners in the engine rooms of the former Soviet economy. In reality, he has the *illusion* of control . . . In fact, you really *are* in control when thousands upon thousands of people, unbeknownst to you, are taking initiatives, going beyond job descriptions and the constraints of their box on the organisation chart, to serve the customer better . . .

Authority and accountability in the Learning Organisation are more widely shared than in the old hierarchies where approvals and authorisations were the privilege of senior managers. Few businesses today can afford double-checking procedures that add no direct value, and people at the front line usually know a great deal more about what is required for customers than an isolated senior manager. These time-wasting approval processes are therefore slowly disappearing.

However, particularly for a manager who may have spent the last 20 years operating a highly controlled environment, the empowerment of others may feel like a large risk to run. Won't we lose control of the business? Won't people be bound to do foolish things?

Today's leaders and the people who work with them need to base their working relationship on a very fundamental value: trust. Handy describes it as having to base working relationships on an 'assumption of competence', whereas in the past we have built whole organisational structures and bureaucratic processes on the assumption of *incompetence*. Clearly there is a risk involved – sometimes an individual will not have the skills or knowledge required to achieve a particular objective. However, it is far more costly to implement vast management hierarchies and bureaucratic checking methods than to risk the occasional mistake or failure.

Empowerment: delegation or abdication?

Empowerment is sometimes dismissed as simply a fashionable word for delegation. The relationship between the two concepts is an important one. Delegation has traditionally meant the handing over of a particular task to a subordinate. The general sense of the term 'delegation' is that real accountability still lies with the boss. Empowerment, on the other hand, means giving people accountability for results. It requires delegation of authority in line with the achievement required. It means setting a goal rather than defining the detailed 'how' to reach it. Also, empowerment has less of a hierarchical basis. For example, you might empower one of your peers to pick up one of your customer leads.

After delegating, you would traditionally monitor and review progress. In empowering, you make yourself available if assistance is required. Empowerment means letting go and trusting someone to achieve an agreed goal. It is a much richer form of delegation – delegating not just the task but true authority and accountability.

People who are empowered have to use their brains, make their own decisions, learn from their mistakes; people to whom a task has been delegated have usually had the thinking done for them and therefore do not have the opportunity to learn.

Many organisations have realised to their surprise that empowerment reinforces the need for leadership rather than lessens it. The individual empowered to act must grasp his or her autonomy and accountability with enthusiasm. The leader must give both the direction and the support needed for the individual to succeed. Without direction and support, empowerment is wasted energy.

What's sauce for the goose . . .

Empowering subordinates is really quite simple: it means treating them just as you would wish to be treated. Senior

managers are usually very clear on the degree of empowerment they require from their boss, even if he or she is the
chief executive. They resent being checked up on, they want
the full delegated authority needed to run their business
properly and they want the opportunity to make the decisions
that affect their customers. Strangely, senior managers quite
often view their employees as a completely different species of
human being, who have far more need for direction and far
less ability to make their own decisions. In businesses that rely
on highly skilled people, this 'two-speed' view of the world
is inaccurate and is certainly inappropriate for a Learning
Organisation.

There is the additional danger of the 'pendulum swing': an
empowering leader who disempowers as soon as times get
tough. This makes it clear that trust is only for good times, and
dampens subsequent initiative-taking. Such hypocrisy breeds
great cynicism, yet could be completely avoided by providing
direction and support in difficult times rather than disempower-
ment. A classic example is the old lever of the recruitment ban
– a favourite cost-control mechanism in the 'command-and-
control' model. We have known organisations who will give
their business unit managers full accountability for their business results on the one hand and impose a complete recruitment ban on the other. Yet a business manager may need to
invest heavily in recruitment in order to achieve the agreed
results. Establishing a cost-reduction goal would achieve the
same result and leave the business unit manager empowered to
choose the best way to achieve it.

Combine an environment of trust with a supportive attitude
to mistakes – one that focuses on the learning rather than the
mistake itself – and you will have an organisation that will
inspire loyalty and commitment, as well as one in which people
will enjoy working. By trusting the people closest to the
customer or to the point of impact of decisions, you will ensure
that the customers' needs are better understood and better met
– the primary objective of any Learning Organisation.

POWERPOINT

Do the leaders in your organisation set a clear direction within which people have freedom to determine how best to achieve?

Do leaders only take on tasks that cannot be addressed at levels closer to the customer?

Do they encourage independence of action and actively discourage dependent behaviour?

Do they trust people to be competent and assume they will always do their best?

Coach

We have suggested that empowerment needs to be combined with a supportive environment, such as a positive attitude towards mistakes. Another critical support mechanism is coaching, a skill that is now essential for anyone aspiring to a leadership role. Unlike the old 'command-and-control' regimes, leaders can no longer simply issue orders and rebuke anyone who doesn't follow them. A major element of a leader's added value in the new world is his or her ability to add the most value to the organisation through other people. Leaders therefore need to see themselves as a supporting function to the people working for them. Max De Pree of Herman Miller, for example, encouraged leaders to think of themselves as 'servants'.

Leaders need to be clear on the strengths, weaknesses and aspirations of the people who work with them and consciously aim to build on the strengths and minimise the weaknesses. Leaders are likely to have skills, knowledge and experience which they can pass on to the benefit of others. So often this wealth of experience stays locked away in someone's head, for their personal use only – a real waste and hidden cost for the organisation. Leaders must be able to share their own personal learning to the direct benefit of others who may by struggling with a particular business issue or who may have identified a gap in their own knowledge. They must make it clear to individuals that asking for help and coaching is not a sign of weakness or incompetence but a sign of high standards and an openness to new ideas.

Coaching is very different from simply telling someone the right answer – it is essentially the difference captured in the metaphor that 'it is better to teach people to fish than to give them a fish'.

Coaching takes time. Leaders should find time for:

- holding informal one-on-one or small-group coaching sessions on business direction to put current activities into an overall context
- working with individuals both before and after training and development events to plan and then consolidate the learning
- playing a mentoring role for people with identified leadership potential
- rehearsing major events such as customer presentations by acting as a 'friendly audience' to their employees
- inviting subordinates to 'shadow' them in new situations to provide opportunities for observation.

Unfortunately, if you were to look at most managers' diaries today, you would still find relatively few coaching sessions – and few opportunities taken in the normal course of events to transfer some learning. It is worth adding that coaching should not be a one-way process – leaders should not hesitate to ask for coaching themselves. By making visible the coaching they get themselves – perhaps by working with non-executive directors on their board or getting some personal counselling from an external management consultant – they send a strong signal that asking for help and advice is not a sign of weakness.

Coaching is a prime example of a Learning Organisation in action. Although leaders play a key role in this, coaching needs to be a way of life for everyone in the organisation – it is one of the most direct, rapid and inexpensive ways to share learning.

POWERPOINT

Do leaders within your organisation invest significant time in coaching others?

Do they ask for coaching themselves?

Collaborator

Particularly in large, complex organisations, the personal network of contacts of any one individual can be an important contribution to their success. This is especially true for leaders, who increasingly depend on people outside their direct control to make things happen. With many critical skills in short supply, a leader needs to have the ability to identify where resources exist that might help achieve a specific objective. This may be in other parts of the organisation or external to it.

The ability to manage joint ventures and alliances is a skill increasingly required. Alliances between competitors is becoming a common feature of organisational life – requiring considerable flexibility and role clarity. In addition, as businesses start to look like Handy's 'Shamrock Organisation', with a core group managing a whole range of subcontractors and a flexible workforce, the number of types of relationship that a leader has to manage increases considerably. A good networker thrives in this environment; an empire-builder feels somewhat uncomfortable.

Resolving conflicts

There is always the potential in large organisations for leaders to develop conflicting or overlapping visions from their part of the organisation. There need to be mechanisms to resolve these conflicts. The Harvard Business School's John Kotter believes that 'thick informal networks' are the natural co-ordinating mechanism for leadership roles within a complex organisation. By this he means strong personal links between the key players, each of whom invests time in building and maintaining good collaborative relationships with his or her colleagues. The formal structures that once defined traditional management roles within the bounds of clear job descriptions simply cannot cope with the rate of change we are now experiencing.

At Swedish–Swiss ABB, for example, each European country contains a number of ABB sister-businesses, each part of a global ABB business. The national head of each of those businesses within a given country is estimated to spend close to 50 per cent of his or her time working with peers there discussing the way forward for ABB as a whole in that country. Where are the new business opportunities? Where might the different business strategies overlap or conflict? The country manager plays a co-ordinating role and facilitates the networking between the heads of ABB businesses in that country. These strong networks enable the co-ordination and consensus-building that leads to the 'whole being greater than the sum of the parts'.

Leaders therefore have to be natural networkers who build good working relationships across boundaries into other parts of their own organisation and out into the external world. Trust is again an important value here – organisations are likely to be far nimbler and better able to make more radical changes when the key leaders work together well and can jointly make some of the difficult decisions, such as where to invest or disinvest. The implication here is that leaders must take or be given opportunities to meet and get to know each other well as individuals – hence the weekend retreats or conferences that might once have been prime candidates for a cost-cutting initiative may well prove to be worthwhile investments with a measurable return.

Collaboration and networking outside the organisation is also crucial. In order to maximise cost effectiveness and speed, leaders must be seeking leading-edge ideas and practices that may have been invented elsewhere. Only by keeping their feelers outside their organisation will this be achieved. The infamous 'NIH' (Not Invented Here) attitude – which suggests that only ideas from within an organisation, or worse, from the leader of that organisation, will be acted upon – has become a very expensive way of operating. Leaders must seek to identify all intellectual capital available to them, from whatever source. Thus they can leverage off the learning of many others – and avoid making mistakes that someone else has made.

 **POWERPOINT**

Do leaders in your organisation collaborate effectively with their peers?

Do they look for win–win relationships rather than win–lose?

Are they skilled at managing alliances and joint ventures?

Do they invest time in external and internal networking in order to build contacts and learn from others?

New performance measures

As well as the challenges they are facing to learn and adapt for themselves, leaders have a responsibility to create environments for others within which they can all learn and develop. As positive as this may sound for the human beings within our organisations, it is in fact a matter of economics. The speed of action, cost effectiveness and customer responsiveness required nowadays are so much greater than before that a revolution is needed in the way our organisations operate.

Leaders must embrace the challenge of harnessing the full brainpower available to them. To do any less than this is to waste the principal asset available to them. In a manufacturing environment, a production manager would probably be fired for running the production line at half-speed day after day. Yet leaders in organisations today are rarely measured on their ability to make the best possible use of the skills and knowledge of their most precious resource: people. We need to identify tangible measures of success so that leaders who create strong, continuously learning teams are the leaders who make it to the top of organisations.

In a Learning Organisation leaders should be measured by both qualitative and quantitative business measures. Examples include:

- multi-input feedback processes (see Chapter 4)
- employee opinion survey results
- internal 'Investor in People' audits, according to the UK standard (see Chapter 10)
- investment made in training and development
- cultural audits that measure a manager/leader's support of cultural values (an approach used by Hewlett Packard)
- contribution to organisational learning mechanisms such as knowledge databases
- number of people moved in and out of his or her area for career development.

On the somewhat cynical assumption that 'people do what you inspect, not what you expect', organisations need to continue to develop ways of making leadership capability assessment more tangible and measurable. The very fact that these 'softer' measures are being tracked and evaluated will be a powerful message to the organisation as a whole. It may make our organisations more effective, but it makes the leadership role a less comfortable one. Managers who believe they are entitled to sit in judgement on others while they themselves are beyond being judged as leaders (least of all by their subordinates) are not suited to a Learning Organisation. The pyramid must be inverted – to paraphrase John F. Kennedy, it is not a question of what your employees have done for you but what you have done for your employees.

POWERPOINT

Are your organisation's leaders measured on both qualitative and quantitative business measures?

Routes to the top

The positions at the top of the organisation chart – chief executives, senior managers, presidents, vice-presidents, directors – carry heavy responsibilities, perhaps more so than ever. The high status and high reward of these roles cause ambitious individuals to spend considerable time and effort identifying the behaviour and types of achievement that will put their names on the successors' list.

In different organisations, with different cultures, promotion into leadership roles has meant playing by the rules; respecting the status quo; meeting budgets and deadlines; working the old boy network; delivering on the bottom line; or perhaps being skilled at selling ideas persuasively. Like the difference between the 'espoused values' printed in company literature and the ones that operate in practice, the route to the top is often by very different means from that printed in the career manuals. Many potentially great leaders have undoubtedly been thwarted by the invisible obstacle course of office politics. However, most 'high-potentials' seem to figure the system out, understand the unwritten rules and make the right connections. Like a five-year-old rapidly working out the intricacies of a new computer game, the people who rise to the top often have an innate, intuitive ability to pick up the signals, learn what the organisation expects of them and to conform. Nancy Foy puts it this way in *Empowering People at Work*:

> The signals employees listen to from top leadership are the same as the ones they listen to from other levels: Who gets hired? Who gets fired? Why?

Today's high-flyers have a particularly difficult challenge as the whole nature of the playing field is changing. The steady steps up a ladder of management levels are being replaced by a requirement to increase personal value – to seek learning opportunities that increase *personal capability* rather than grades that enhance *personal status*. Power in organisations is now a question of harnessing as much brainpower as possible to complex business issues; it is no longer a question of control but of co-ordination and empowerment of others.

Current leaders, whose careers were founded on building empires they could 'command and control', need to be aware that promoting in their own image may be quite the opposite of what their organisation needs as sea changes take place in their markets. The Learning Organisation would look for a variety of inputs on 'high potential' for leadership roles rather than rely on a hierarchical process of recommendation. Assessment against the *values* of the organisation may be as important as evidence of results achievement. Certainly the latter, often considered as evidence enough, is insufficient for leading a Learning Organisation.

Having outlined the characteristics that you believe leaders will need in your Learning Organisation, the crucial task of identifying and developing people with these qualities must be undertaken. ICL has for a number of years used a process known as the Organisation and Management Review (OMR) – one of the few corporate processes across a devolved organisation, and one that is directly linked to business plans. Each business unit identifies the individuals seen to have senior management potential; the career development of those individuals is then discussed and facilitated at company level by a board composed of managing directors of several different major ICL businesses. Other organisations invest in full-time attention to this vital area, such as Philips of the Netherlands with its Corporate Staff Bureau.

You must have a formal process which identifies the talent that will give your organisation a future. Whichever process you decide is right for your organisation, you will need to review regularly the criteria you are using to identify future leaders. To illustrate the changes that have taken place in recent years, you have only to compare the new leadership criteria we are suggesting with the set of criteria traditionally applied to managerial roles, namely the ability to *plan, organise* and *control.*

You will also need to consider the different leadership roles within your organisation and where the emphasis might need to be in terms of criteria. As a general rule, the more senior the role, the more of an emphasis there will be on being a visionary and a risk-taker. The other four characteristics – coach, learner, empowerer and collaborator – are equally important in leadership roles at all levels. The traditional management skills, which could perhaps be summarised as project or task management skills, become more important as you move away from strategy-setting roles towards implementation roles.

Having identified the individuals who show promise for leadership roles, you must ensure that they are provided with learning opportunities with the right amount of stretch and challenge.

There are a number of processes which can be used:

- Action learning approaches – working in teams on real company issues and perhaps presenting recommendations to the board of directors – are an excellent methodology for giving people with potential for senior leadership roles the opportunity to develop strategic thinking skills. Such approaches, particularly if they involve current senior managers, are also a good way to increase the visibility of the people with leadership potential.
- Career guidance events which help them reflect on their strengths and weaknesses and identify the most appropriate career path are another mechanism which can assist individuals in planning their learning to reach senior roles.
- Secondments and assignments to provide specific opportunities for learning, based on a high-potential individual's knowledge or skill gaps, should be planned.

- Consortium programmes or business school events can give people with leadership potential the opportunity to benchmark and learn from peers in other organisations.

However, a Learning Organisation must also accept that new styles and approaches are sometimes better 'bought' than 'made' – there must also be room for hiring in leaders/ managers to bring fresh perspectives and approaches to the management culture of the organisation.

This new emphasis on the people-related traits of leaders, such as coaching and collaboration, brings to the fore some of the traits more typically associated with women rather than men. It is likely that we will see more women move into senior leadership roles as organisations call for these 'feminine' skills and approaches. In any case, the identification and promotion of people such as we have described is likely to make our organisations both more fulfilling and more challenging places to work. Fulfilling, because people can stretch their capability; challenging, because there is no room for passengers who are not prepared to keep learning to stay ahead of the changes that surround them.

 **POWERPOINT**

Do the people who are promoted into leadership roles clearly demonstrate the characteristics of the Learning Organisation leader?

Have you established a mangement development framework that focuses on increasing personal value and is clearly understood by everyone?

Do the top leaders in your organisation recognise the need for a new profile of leadership qualities to be articulated and supported?

Does the organisation invest in a planned, specific way to the leadership development of high-potential individuals?

Are people recruited from outside into selected roles to bring new perspectives to the organisation?

Pointers for action

A new style of leadership does not develop overnight. Many organisations will live for some time to come with the reality of senior managers of the 'old school' who will be unmoved by many of the arguments we have put forward for a new way of thinking. Like any elephant-sized task, it will need to be broken into bite-sized chunks. We would suggest that some first steps might be as follows:

- Train your existing managers in coaching and facilitation skills.
- Create self-development-oriented workshops to give managers the opportunity to reflect and act on their changing business and own development needs.
- Agree a new set of criteria for promotion into leadership roles, based on the business challenges you expect to face in coming years.
- Publish a set of capability profiles for leaders.
- Ensure you have a process for identifying and developing the people with potential for leadership roles.
- Recruit some new people of your ideal profile into one or two key leadership roles.
- Pilot some innovative ways of measuring leadership effectiveness in receptive parts of your organisation.

The high-flyers of the 1990s who will take our organisations well into the 21st century must above all be fast learners. They must adapt quickly to new customer requirements, move quickly to take new market opportunities, and learn how to galvanise people into action when their formal authority over them may be minimal. Like a guided missile constantly correcting its course until it hits the target, they must learn from their mistakes and stay on course. Any organisation that still rewards and promotes by the old rules is unlikely to have the leadership capability to carry it into the next century.

3

The Power of Language and Culture

The way we do things around here

The potential power of a Learning Organisation is wholly dependent on a supportive organisational culture. 'Culture' means the way things are done, the personality and behaviour of the organisation. Just as changing behaviour and assumptions may be a painstaking and painful process for people, so it is for organisations. The culture is the product of many influences – history, location, heroes, myths, current personalities – and is a collection of written, but mainly unwritten, 'rules'. Many change programmes or mergers between different organisations fail because the power of cultures is underestimated. Likewise individuals making job changes find integration into new cultures the toughest change to manage, and some organisations never seem to be able to keep late entrants beyond a 'polite' period. Virgin Atlantic once hired a senior executive from British Airways, and he lasted only three days – the unstructured, personality-driven Virgin was too much to adapt to.

As we have noted before, learning is happening all the time, but often inefficiently, accidentally and without being applied effectively for the good of both the individual and the organisation. The values and behaviours that make up the culture play an essential role in enabling or blocking the development of a continuously improving Learning Organisation. National cultures naturally influence and overlay any organisational cultures; a Learning Organisation is judged by its results, and they may be achieved in quite different ways in the USA, in Germany or in Japan. Some basic tenets probably apply universally, however.

Many organisations in the 1990s are undergoing major changes that challenge basic assumptions of structure, roles and rewards. Some of these changes are as upsetting, confusing and security-challenging as those experienced by people in the Russian republics when central control and provision disappeared. The cushions of comfort are being withdrawn. We discuss in Chapter 8 (on organisational learning) the effects of different *structures* in supporting the Learning Organisation, but let us say now that many of the changes under the heading of 'organisational transformation' fundamentally support such a culture. The concept of 'empowerment' has different meanings to different people, but any moves to what Charles Handy summarises as 'encouraging curiosity, trust, forgiveness and togetherness' instead of 'rigidity, hierarchy and bureaucracy' must boost learning. An empowering and devolved culture releases energy, experimentation, accountability and initiative. A team-based structure gives flexibility and fluidity, with people being able to increase and share their learning naturally.

It is not all good news, however. The more an organisation fragments into divisions and teams, the less easy it is to ensure that knowledge is shared and utilised across all the boundaries. The natural rivalries that emerge in organisations are likely to be greater rather than less. There are assumptions that people *want* to be empowered and take decisions for themselves – not always so! Also there is a real threat to traditional managers of turning on its head much of what they have been trained for and told over the years; it is natural there will be resistance to perceived insecurity.

This area we feel has been much underestimated in the literature on Learning Organisations, and we have split it into two chapers – one concerned with *behaviour* (this chapter) and the other with *processes* (Chapter 4).

The way we learn around here

Have you ever thought about this question in your organisation? To take one extreme, do you consider that learning is the job of the training department, and – depending on the money available – that people should be sent solely on courses each year? Or do you see learning as a thread running through everything you do, every day? The power from learning in organisations *is* in understanding that last question. It isn't just to be focused on more creative and interesting learning opportunities for individuals. It is a permeating lifestream that people care about, think about, talk about and organise to maximise. We are after a culture that fully supports learning in every sense.

In empowered, flexible and rules-free organisations, is it feasible to mandate a learning framework that is *beyond* the unit level? Are we not dependent on each unit leader embracing for themselves the values, systems and processes that will maximise learning for the good of all? This cannot be answered in any universal way, since different organisations must find different answers. In our discussion we will assume that it is at least *beneficial* to all parties to share in a culture that crosses the boundaries of the organisation.

In Chapter 1 we recommmended creating a 'blueprint' of characteristics that you believe to be appropriate to your organisation. This would include some descriptions of the desired cultural behaviours.

We start with a firm belief in what Alan Mumford calls 'everyday learning' – and this takes us away immediately from any assumption that learning is separable from the tasks that are performed in our organisations. Peter Honey advocates that some rules should become institutionalised for the following reasons:

- *People rarely do more than they need to.* 'Discretionary' things nearly always have a habit of being only laudable intentions under the pressures of organisational life and therefore get left out. This would include taking the time to learn from experiences, disciplined coaching and giving feedback, long-term planning, and self-management.
- *'Good' behaviour should never be assumed.* The fear of failure and reprisals leads to people spending time and effort

to 'keep their head down', and so there needs to be positive encouragement of good learning behaviours.
* *In most organisations upward deference is rife*. People have a tendency to tell superiors what they want to hear, and to be economical with unpleasant news. Thus the lessons that might be learnt from events and experience may be suppressed. David Megginson of the Sheffield Business School calls this the difficulty of 'speaking truth to power'.

We could add a number of other anti-Learning Organisation behaviours; some of them are discussed below. But we are not so sure that rules can be institutionalised by decree! Rather, we must understand the elements of culture that are necessary to enable a Learning Organisation to flourish, and what changes we need to introduce to our culture in order to make progress.

Again, we need to note the differing approaches of different national cultures. Has the indifference to 'MBA'-type programmes by Japan and Germany yielded better or worse economic progress? We could conclude that their success makes an excellent case for the abandonment of such programmes. Mills and Friesen quote the example of Honda, who rotate young engineers through the Formula One racing team that they sponsor in order to teach them 'the racing competitive spirit' and the need for innovative, speedy decisions on the spot. Honda do not believe any business school can teach this through the classroom.

Not only do individuals learn in different ways, but they may be *conditioned* through their culture to be oriented towards certain styles. The West generally values systematic rationality and programmed learning; the East, harmonious concepts and ideals and intuitive learning. Joost Muller and Diana Watts of the De Baak Management Study Centre in the Netherlands looked at the Learning Organisation concept in different countries. Japan and America present contrasting 'systematic' and 'systemic' approaches. Muller and Watts credit the British, meanwhile, with being the first to explore the strategic concept but claim that they 'are not strong on learning across boundaries'.

The Netherlands and Scandinavia are traditionally supportive of the human side of organisations, and have embraced and explored (particularly in Sweden) many social aspects of the Learning Organisation. In Germany there is a movement to learn from the Anglo-American approaches, even though their learning philosophy is rigorously academic, followed by practical experience. Thomas Sattelberger, while at Deutsche Aerospace, brought together a number of German and English thinkers in his book *Die Lernende Organisation* ('The Learning Organisation') – his own contributions linking clearly with structural and cultural transformation.

Cultural elements

The ones we have chosen for discussion as being most relevant to our purpose are:

- *values and beliefs* – 'having a creed'
- *language* – how people talk about learning
- *messages, expectations and behaviour from senior management* – what they say and do
- *norms of behaviour* – what's 'OK' and 'not OK'
- *commitment to time and money*
- *ownership of learning*
- *politics, sharing and NIH (Not Invented Here)*.

We discuss in Chapter 4 the human resource policies and processes that are necessary to support and complete the culture.

 **POWERPOINT**

Does the organisation have a defined and communicated approach to learning?

Is the culture in your organisation one that explicitly or implicitly supports a *range* of learning behaviours?

Having a creed

Values and beliefs exist in all organisations – there are of course the 'written' and 'unwritten' ones. On the one hand we may hear senior executives avowing publicly that their most precious asset is their people. And yet not so far down in the organisation we may be told that 'costs go around on two legs', and the accountants are obsessed with counting headcount – as if that was ever a relevant measure of assets in a flexibly resourced organisation. It comes down to a fundamental creed: 'Do we really regard people as an *investment* or as a *cost*?' People themselves can actually tell you how they feel treated – in fact, this is a good question for opinion surveys!

Whereas the unwritten values change slowly, and are heavily influenced by the messages and behaviours coming from top management, we believe there is real merit in having a statement of *espoused* values – 'the way we would like to be'. Though they may be viewed cynically to start with, they provide a benchmark for behaviour and practices, something to strive for, and are essential in marking out a culture change. It is highly likely that they will include references to customers, quality, excellence, and so on. There are very few we have seen that pick out the importance of continuous learning, or its equivalent. Until recently, that is: newly formulated value statements are including it. An example was provided in 1993 by the Nokia Group of Finland, who in formulating their 'Nokia Way' chose:

- customer satisfaction
- respect for the individual
- achievement
- continuous learning.

The corporate slogan is defined as:

'Nokia – Connecting People'.

Nokia's CEO, Jorma Ollila, whose 1993 Annual Report entitled 'Forward with Strong Values' we mentioned earlier, says that 'In the Nokia Group, knowledge is power only when it is shared'.

When ICL as part of its renaissance in the early 1980s put together its 'ICL Way' it included in the seven commitments of every employee a 'Commitment to People Development'. Some of the supporting statements were as follows:

> Our commitment to achievement demands a commitment to develop our skills and abilities in every possible way. We are a people Company. Our main strength comes from the quality and skill of the people who work here. So real progress will come about only by constantly developing and improving our skills. People development is a key to business success. Managers carry an obligation to respond to and encourage employees . . .

The 'ICL Way' also included 'Ten Obligations of Every Manager', and amongst these were teamwork, developing people, innovation and self-measurement. These have stood the test of time, and were reissued as an integral part of a new statement of cultural direction entitled 'The Management Framework' in 1992.

Of course such statements do not cause change in themselves, but they serve as vital anchor points to be referenced in policies, processes and communications which eventually define 'what we want to be known for'. We would expect the Learning Organisation to have such a statement in its value statements, for example:

CONTINUOUS LEARNING

> We believe in the vital importance of the skills and abilities of all our resources, whether employees, suppliers or other partners. We will encourage and support policies and activities that ensure their continuous development, and ways of sharing knowledge and experience for the good of all. We will listen carefully to our customers and their

needs, and in every aspect of our business will benchmark ourselves against the best organisations externally.

How are these statements used? They should be:

- made visible and available to every employee
- referred to and quoted in speeches of senior people both internally and externally
- referred to in written policies
- quoted and explored in learning programmes.

Too often, such values remain for a long time as *intentions*. The extent to which they match the *real* values in practice at any point in time is seen in the areas discussed in the following sections.

 **POWERPOINT**

Does the organisation have a set of values which includes:

– a commitment to continuous learning for individuals and teams?

– the sharing of knowledge and experience in the organisation for the benefit of all?

– the desire to be a competitive Learning Organisation?

How people talk about it

Capability

Every organisation has a language of its own that conveys its messages. A Learning Organisation needs a shared set of words which talk about the 'capability' of people, and reinforce the messages of learning that we need. The popular term for the 1990s is 'competencies'. This is a rather generic term, however, and can mean quite different things to different people. We prefer the breakdown into:

- *knowledge* – what someone knows
- *skills* – what someone can do
- *attitudes* – the beliefs that shape how they do things
- *experience* – what someone has actually done.

We add experience for two reasons: first, because most learning comes from doing and therefore experience is the most important part of a person's 'portfolio', and second, because the *context* in which a competence has been learnt is important. For example, one could say one knows how to do 'financial budgeting'. But it is easy to see the difference between budgeting for a small-cost centre and budgeting for a complex operation with several revenue streams.

Some wonder about the inclusion of *attitudes*. There may not be too many factors here, but they can be crucially important. One such is the willingness to learn. People, and organisations, have mental blocks here – caused maybe by having their fingers burnt through experimentation, by complacency or arrogance, or by just not seeing the value to be obtained. Most attitudinal blocks can be overcome by resetting the heart and mind, using education and discussion.

As for *knowledge* and *skills*, it is also helpful to define *levels* of competence. These are defined in great detail in the UK in the work of the Management Charter Initiative and the definition of National Vocational Qualifications – such analysis may or may not be helpful in your organisation. We feel the principle of distinguishing levels of know-how, typically in five stages from 'awareness' to 'expert', is helpful.

The sum of these four elements for an individual makes up their accumulated learning or 'Personal Growth Profile', the term used by Mayo in *Managing Careers*. Such language enables us to give some precision to the definition of learning objectives and to choosing experiences or new roles in a way that matches the individual profile, or the next learning needs.

The same principle may apply to a team or organisation, as they look at their levels of competence and learning needs.

This language of 'capability' will be reflected throughout the people management processes in the organisation, as discussed in Chapter 4. Examples are the description of roles and their requirements, analysis of personal or team performance, design of learning plans, and selection criteria.

Learning

The use of the word 'learning' itself is a key cultural influence. We will distinguish between *education*, *training*, and *learning*.

Education is the exposure to new knowledge, concepts and ideas in a relatively programmed way. It is normally aimed at increasing *knowledge*, or in modifying *attitudes* and beliefs. It is aimed at broadening the 'mindset' of a person, and this is particularly hard to evaluate and assess. A typical example is an 'executive education' event which focuses on exposing the mind to ideas and models, and to the experiences of other organisations.

Training covers those solutions to a learning need which involve being taught or shown a way of doing things; it is essentially *skills*-oriented. Such skills may be motor skills, or they may be behavioural. Both areas can be dealt with either by on-the-job coaching or by off-the-job programmes; the latter is prevalent, no doubt due to the fact that they are easier to partake in and organise. Wherever possible, on-the-job or action-oriented approaches to skill development should be evaluated first in looking for the appropriate solution.

The term *learning* is 'student-need-centred' and starts with the beneficiary. It can be argued that it is an output, and indeed in the structure of our model of the Learning Organisation we see it as a 'result' rather than an 'enabler' (see page 235). It provides an open framework of thinking which begins and ends with the real need rather than a particular solution. Thus we would want to be talking about 'learning needs' and 'learning objectives', 'learning solutions and methodologies', 'learning plans', and 'learning evaluation'. It helps us to understand that people learn in different ways, and to choose solutions and resources accordingly. We will be thinking of the range of people who assist in the learning process rather then be separating out 'trainers' as a special type of resource. Every person in the organisation needs to be a 'trainer' in the sense of a 'helper of others in their learning'.

When mistakes occur, do we naturally revert to macho language describing them in heavily negative tones? Or do we talk in terms of 'lessons to be learned'?

Names and titles

This use of language also needs to be applied in all the various processes for human resource development throughout the organisation. The way departments and job titles are designated also gives a message. Is it appropriate to have a 'training department'? Only if it is seen as part of a broader context of activities and contributions to the Learning Organisation. So, organisations are increasingly changing such terms. ICL calls its old staff-training department 'ICL Learning' and its members 'Learning Consultants'; BP's director in charge of people development is called 'Head of Learning and Development'.

More subtle messages can be communicated by the use of language. We mentioned earlier the way headcount is sometimes used, as if it is something that goes up and down like the number of computer terminals. Referring to expenditure on training as being in the class of 'deferrable expense items' lets people know how important it is seen to be. We support the UK Government in choosing the term 'Investors in People' for their certification scheme in people development standards, for the message the word 'investors' gives. (ICL, as it happened, called their performance and development programme 'Investing in People' some years earlier, and still calls it that.)

How do we refer to employees? Does our language give a

message that each is an individual, or that they are merely a resource to be utilised? How do we speak about contractual help – 'contractors' or 'partners/associates'? Do our job titles reflect the kind of organisation we seek – for example, 'team leaders' rather than 'supervisors', or 'quality consultants' rather than 'quality managers'? Is 'managing director' a title that is appropriate in Learning Organisations?

 **POWERPOINT**

Is there a common language about capability that meets the needs of your organisation, and is used throughout the relevant people-management processes?

Is the term 'learning' in common currency, and is it used in such a way that good learning practices are supported?

What the top people say and do

The messages, expectations and behaviour from senior managers are powerful indicators of what is treated *seriously* 'around here'. We do not expect most senior management to talk in the language or jargon of professionals in human resource development, or to discuss at length the merits and characteristics of the Learning Organisation. Nevertheless we could reasonably hope that they have seen the importance of the arguments in Chapter 1, and espouse for themselves the basic principles. Moreover, we legitimately expect them to 'live the values' where these have been made explicit.

People soon pick up whether senior management sees them primarily as a cost or an investment, whether they are being *used* or *valued*. So one looks for consistent messages which support the need for continuous learning, and which make clear to the levels of management below that competitive investment and effort are expected.

Managers are easily turned off by inappropriate 'evangelism' on behalf of people working in human resource management, especially with the plethora of new jargon coming from management 'gurus'. The inherent competitive advantages to be had from the Learning Organisation may therefore be overshadowed. Managers have a right to expect to understand the objectives of the organisation sufficiently well in order to give intelligent and realistic help towards their achievement.

The role of the *top team* is important in acting in a concerted way to establish the values of a Learning Organisation. Bob Garratt in *Creating a Learning Organisation* gives five key conditions the team needs to consider:

- clear formulation of strategy and policy
- taking time and space to think and learn themselves
- demonstrating their own willingness to learn from each other as a team
- delegating problem-solving operational issues to others rather than trying to handle them themselves
- setting a climate that encourages continuous learning at all levels.

People are quick to detect dissonance in a top team, and it is always a major challenge to be seen to take 'cabinet responsibility' for decisions. To be seen to be learning from one another and together is an extremely powerful message.

Most managers below the senior levels respond first to the immediate pressures of the day, month or quarter, and it is foolish to expect otherwise. Since much learning has a longer pay-off it is always going to be a battle to find time to give the right emphasis on it. Logic is not enough here. People development advisers can make it easy for managers to play their rightful role in the Learning Organisation through giving responsive, credible and practical advice at the right time; they should give a range of choices for learning solutions and especially options for coaching for the manager to use.

All leaders play a key role in this cultural arena. There are a number of tests that show the level of commitment; we list some of the questions we could ask as a 'Powerpoint':

POWERPOINT

When times are hard or 'end-of-year' financial pressures are heavy, is the budget for learning still protected?

Do senior leaders show concern for the level of spending and resourcing for learning in relation to competition?

Do senior leaders actively push the specialists in the organisation to explore new ways of learning?

Do senior leaders look for opportunities to mention the importance of continuous shared learning in speeches, inspirational letters, company newsletters and other forms of communication?

Do senior leaders build items relating to learning achievements into objective-setting and reward schemes?

What's 'OK' and 'not OK'

What the 'values statement' says, and what the chief executive says he or she wants are often *ahead* of the real culture. Reality is about the way people actually behave, and what is seen as acceptable or otherwise. We quoted Peter Honey earlier taking a pessimistic view of the ability to establish a learning culture without reinforcement by 'rules'. Formalised processes have a powerful influence on how managers behave, but especially in a devolved, empowered and rapidly changing environment the scope for individual interpretation must be high.

Things that need to be 'OK' and accepted as such by everyone include:

- an open communication climate where mistakes can be admitted and discussed as learning experiences, as opposed to being subjects for punishment

- planning for time to be spent in personal and team learning
- expecting to receive information, help and advice from others
- ensuring it is not only acceptable, but required, to learn from other departments and to share freely knowledge and experience
- the use of learning opportunities rather than an individual's previous knowledge as the basis for deciding who should take part in a working group or go on a visit
- demonstrating and reinforcing the fact that the NIH (Not Invented Here) syndrome is 'not OK'
- not just tolerating but encouraging the questioning of assumptions and processes
- a culture of feedback – people should look for it, take it constructively and respond when asked to provide it
- the encouragement of experimentation and innovation at all levels.

⚡ POWERPOINT

Does your organisation have a shared understanding of the behaviours that are, and those that are not, supportive of a continuous learning climate?

Does it use this to check from time to time whether people in the organisation believe such behaviours are supported in reality?

Are behaviours which are clearly against the agreed set discussed with the individual concerned?

Time and money

There are few messages as powerful as time and money, and how they are allocated. Is our use of them supporting what we believe and what we say we want to do? Since much of the power of the Learning Organisation lies in recognising how to harness systematically the vast array of learning opportunities available to us, it is often time that is the premium rather than money. Time is demanded for:

- making and reviewing learning plans for self and staff
- reviewing the day's events and work-based learning
- benchmarking internally and externally
- giving and receiving feedback
- researching and accessing what other people know
- communicating what we know to others
- coaching and mentoring
- personal experimentation and innovation
- personal knowledge and skill enhancement – keeping up to date.

We spend our entire days in learning-related activities, even though they may not be specified like those in the above list; what is missing from the list is this natural learning from everyday work, which is not measured in time or money. However, some 'formal' recognisable activities supportive to learning are necessary. The difference between the messages 'do you really have to spend time on that now?' and 'this is an opportunity for learning we cannot afford to miss' is easily discerned.

The need to mandate some processes as a normal, everyday part of the 'way we do things around here' is, perhaps sadly, a practical compromise.

Most of the listed activities do not cost in any significant way. However, many learning activities do have to be budgeted for – courses, seminars, visits, materials and so on. We would perhaps not spend so much if we were able to maximise the everyday learning opportunities. When organisations compare and benchmark with others, they will look at the cost of training department and courses, probably including accommodation but not salary costs of trainees. In France the government lays down figures that must be reported by every organisation in its *bilan social*, or annual return on personnel statistics, including items such as total training spend, training spend as a percentage of costs, amount spent per employee, and details of apprentices and trainees.

The question here of course is: how 'sacrosanct' is the budget for learning? Is it a candidate for cutting when pressures come, or is it to be regarded as essential expenditure? The emphasis that is emerging on the competitive advantage of employee skills is causing managers to think more carefully before cutting back. The committed Learning Organisation would of course resist heavily any cut-back in such vital investment. One can argue also that *annual* budgets are inappropriate in an organisation that operates in a turbulent environment and is adapting constantly to it; *rolling* budgets are much to be preferred.

One area of expenditure is the investment in 'learning consultancy'. To what extent does a manager understand his or her need for specialist help on learning, and the options available? Is that help available through traditional human resource departments? Sadly, there are all too few skilled practitioners on the people development side, as career progress in the function has focused on generalist experience. Many organisations outsource for expertise, and there is no shortage of consultants! There is undoubtedly a balance to be found between internal and external capability.

We would argue for an internal capability where the organisation:

- is heavily involved in change programmes and collective learning which is strategic
- requires shifts in capability across several divisions
- wants to reinforce its core values in a consistent way
- wants to learn from its accumulated wisdom and experience and share that through learning events.

Bringing in consultant capability from outside is often a good option, but every consultant has their own solutions and language. A mark of capability is the consultant who finds a solution unique to your organisation using *your* language.

POWERPOINT

Does your organisation encourage people to invest time in continuous and job-related learning activities?

Is there a defined learning budget, owned at the lowest level in the organisation?

Is the learning budget regarded as a key investment and non-tradeable?

The power of ownership

'Learning', even if so called, would be regarded traditionally as the job of the training department. Organisations differ in their approach to who pays for what, and it is fashionable in the UK at the time of writing to have market-determined approaches to internal services, where the internal training function competes with external suppliers.

There are two questions here: who owns the learning of individuals, and who owns collective learning? Let us define ownership as *accountability to see that things happen.*

Individual learning

Most appraisal systems have put the emphasis firmly on the manager as the person responsible for the development of his or her employees. This has implied that he or she owns the development plans, and is accountable for making them happen. A simplistic approach to development built around training courses means this is little more than choosing some events that are hopefully appropriate, and organising the release of people for them.

The power of a Learning Organisation is in the breadth and depth of the opportunities for learning that is sees and exploits. It recognises that most learning occurs through practical job experience, and clearly the manager holds the key to a large portion of that. We assume, somewhat optimistically, that he or she is capable of finding the time for coaching and incidental learning lessons, and is equipped with the required personal skills. But on-the-job learning is not dependent on the manager alone: colleagues, peers, subordinates or external contacts may be part of the learning process. Who should own this complex web? – *The person in the centre of it!*

The individual should own their personal learning objectives and learning plans, and make these dynamic and self-renewing. The processes we might use to do this are described in Chapter 4. But the principle is important. It implies that:

- as an individual I do not expect the organisation primarily to manage my career or my learning; I acknowledge that it is in my interest to enhance my personal value and to look after both my internal and my external continuing employability;
- I need a lot of support from my manager, who can allocate funds to me, empower me to manage my time between learning experiences and work achievements, and can be a coach to me in passing on his or her own experiences or help me through certain job-related experiences;
- I need the support of the organisation as well: I want to be recognised for my increased value through learning; both my manager and I can benefit from expertise in the management of learning from a specialist; and I need to be able to tap into databases of learning opportunities relevant to the organisation I work in to enable me to make good choices.

There is a triangle of contribution here, as shown in Figure 3.1.

The traditional roles and required competencies of each party may be viewed as follows:

Figure 3.1
Triangle of contribution to learning

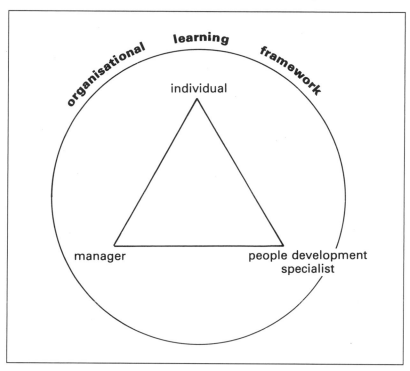

Manager: role as controller of feedback and learning opportunities has changed to that of coach and helper. Needs to be competent in understanding how people learn; helping to set learning objectives; scheduling work assignments with learning opportunities in mind; coaching and counselling; opening doors and sharing experience.

Individual: Role as receiver of plans for development has changed to that of owner of personal growth. Needs to understand own learning style; be disciplined in reviewing learning from everyday experiences; be open in seeking and responding to feedback; and take decisions in management of personal time and priorities.

People development specialist: Role as guardian of the administrative processes and course-booker has changed to that of consultant and facilitator of learning solutions. Needs real expertise in learning styles and methods; ability to advise on choices; and to be a consultant on all aspects of the learning process.

We should note of course that there are many other contributors to an individual's *learning*; but we see those described above as the contributors to the learning plan.

Many of these skills will need considerable development themselves to be effective. We should note that this is empowerment in action, and some organisations have gone so far as to give a sum of money (typically in the UK between £300 and £1,000) for the individual to spend on their development as they feel best. This is an integral part of defining a new culture, and needs to be part of a managed cultural change programme. It involves a change in the pyschological contract between individuals and the organisation.

Collective learning

An organisation is an impersonal entity and cannot itself own the learning within it. A part of the entity needs to own that learning on its behalf. (In a perfect world that would mean a dispersed responsibility shared by all its parts.) But reality is never perfect – otherwise one would never need auditors.

An organisation needs both a champion for learning and a programme manager. The former should be the chief executive and the latter someone such as the director of human resources, if one exists, since he or she owns so many of the supportive policies and processes. Supporting the owners would ideally be a centre of expertise in learning itself. (The role that might be played by such a resource is discussed in our final chapter.)

To do this requires commitment to some resources. It seems to us to be a big mistake to avoid any central resource in this area just because the prevailing religion is to have a minimalist headquarters for its own sake. The development of the learning capability of the organisation and the people in it is a fundamental business concern, as we show elsewhere, and a vital part of *corporate synergy*. This is real added value and plays a critical role in the effective Learning Organisation.

 **POWERPOINT**

Is it clear to all individuals that they need personally to own their learning?

Do the supporting processes emphasise and empower such ownership?

Is there an organisational champion and programme leader of Learning Organisation principles?

Pride and prejudice

It has been said that an organisation cannot learn – only the people in it can. This is dangerous, because there *are* organisations that have found ways to share knowledge and maximise individual learning for the benefit of all. The secret of comparative competitive advantage lies in the question: what is our capability to *transfer* and *make available to all* the learning of individuals so that the organisation as a whole is richer and more capable?

Many writers have concentrated on the learning of individuals as the key to the Learning Organisation, but Swieringa and Wierdsma point out very clearly that 'organisational learning only occurs if, as a result of one person learning, others operate differently'. At its basic level, this requires sharing knowledge and experience – and this is a matter of cultural support in terms of *supporting systems* and *mutual expectancy*.

A football team cannot survive on the capabilities of each

individual being allowed to blossom independently of the needs of the team. What is it that creates something greater than the individual members themselves? They share some common aims which, if achieved, will be to common benefit. These aims may cause personal ones to be suppressed. The players share information and experience freely. They abide by some disciplines for the good of all. They constantly watch other teams and see how well they do things. They learn and unlearn movements and set-pieces that will enable them to be winners.

So it is with organisations. Unfortunately, the larger the organisation is, the more 'tribalism' and power games may operate against the common good. *Information is power*, and subdivisions, teams and individuals like to keep it to themselves. But an organisation needs to learn. It needs to create a residue of knowledge and wisdom that is greater than that held by the individuals in it.

Andrew Kakabadse in his study *Politics in Management* discusses the differences in motivation and self-interest that cause inevitable clashes between, for example, headquarters and divisions, management and workers, or between structural units. Conflicts and alliances, pressure groups and hidden deals all result. The way individuals approach unknown and threatening areas is based on their accumulated experiences (ie learning) of what is in their interest and what is not. They quickly learn how powerful information can be. To cite an example, a colleague had the opportunity to move from personnel management – a relatively open type of function, where information is readily shared – to being the leader of a software production and marketing department. The time came to explain to a new chief executive where he stood on his development projects. He was honest, telling him how late we would be, and why. The atmosphere was frosty, and from that day forward there was a lack of confidence in the department. When he asked the direct boss what mistake had been made, he sighed and said, 'George, you *must* learn not to tell everything you know!'

The nature of tribalism in organisations

Wherever people live and work together they form 'tribal' alliances, and in organisations these have a substantial influence on the overall culture. As we have learnt from Maslow's needs hierarchy, the need for 'security' requires continual satisfaction for most people, especially those whose 'career anchor' (Schein) naturally leads them to work together with others towards common purposes. Loyalty to the 'tribe' can override self-interest, and has a natural tendency to be greater than that to the organisation as a whole. Tribes form their own codes of conduct and values; have spokesmen and representatives; meet together on matters of common interest; may fight together for their rights; and, most importantly, have their own rules about the *ownership*, *sharing* and *distribution of information*.

Individuals normally have several tribal loyalties, some of which are stronger than others. Thus one may at the same time belong to national, functional, status, and 'origin-based' tribes. Such loyalties may not all be equal. People change tribes, and it is often amazing how loyalties and priorities (once fiercely held) change to gain speedy acceptance in the new situation. Underneath there are always loyalties that may be more important than one's current position in the organisation.

In small family or entrepreneurial organisations the difference between the 'owning' tribe and others can be most acute. But in organisations of every size, to understand where someone may be positioning themselves it is important to study the 'colour of the head-dress' – in other words, what it means to be 'one of us'.

Some of the types of tribe that exist may include:

* *those based on **status** differences*. Organisations create these through their benefit structures, dress codes and dining arrangements. The classic case is seen in the 'trade union v the management' divide. A modern Learning Organisation would seek to discourage such differences, and recognise

that every contributor is important to the success of the enterprise, regardless of their role. Trust is achieved by open information; although the UK has its own informal systems, consultation and communication have been mandated between management and employees in different ways in most European countries.

- *those derived from **constituent components** of an organisation that has grown inorganically through mergers and acquisitions.* These are very powerful especially in the years following the absorption. Clubs of former members may be maintained for many years, and reunions are well attended. One of us was recently invited to a reunion to celebrate 10 years since the disbandment of a particular subsidiary in a reorganisation. Word spread internally and externally; 300 people attended, from previous managing directors to post-room helpers, all bringing some momento of this enjoyable organisation they had worked for. Such tribe members will *always help each other* and share information between themselves.

  The goal here is not to deny the constituent loyalties but, by taking the best from the components, which everyone can identify with. This was done in the case of the merger between Nokia Data and ICL Europe, and has been written up by Mayo and Hadaway in the *Journal of Management Development*.

- *those derived from **national or regional** origin.* Some nationalities have the advantage of their own language, which provides a very effective entry-barrier to would-be tribal members. Yet one of the mistakes many people make is to see only the national boundaries as tribal. Africa is not the only continent where this is clearly not the case – it is true in Europe also. There are the obvious 'tribal' divides between the countries that make up the United Kingdom, but there are also subtler ones within other national boundaries, such as those between Catalonia and Castile in Spain or between northern and southern Italy, and so on. Whether exiled or expatriated, tribal members always form a community of common interest. Different languages and dialects powerfully reinforce the tribe, and information-sharing may be blurred through both cultural and linguistic misunderstandings.

- *those arising from 'divisional' membership in a devolved organisation*. This is the area where change of loyalty can happen with least pain as people cross boundaries. But the height of the fences can be very high. Local interests are often reinforced by the reward systems in place, and by internal competitive pressures, either overt or hidden. The focus on divisional profit targets, for example, becomes a subtle internal competitive force as people maximise their own revenues or minimise their own costs in ways that might not be to the advantage of the organisation as a whole.

  Information is recognised as power, and may be closely guarded. The tribal behaviours from this category can be the most destructive in the pursuit of the Learning Organisation. Charles Handy, in recognising the trend to devolution to smaller units, advocates the search for 'twin citizenship', to enable federal synergy to live in harmony with business divisions.

- *those arising from 'functional' membership*. Thus a person may belong to a functional or professional community which shares qualifications and technical expertise areas, a common interest to be powerful and have influence as a community, and which crosses divisional borders. It is likely there will be a functional leader in 'headquarters' who leads the tribe and is seen as their senior representative. The respective strengths of this kind of loyalty over the earlier 'divisional' type varies; they may be equal, or biased one way or the other. The central role and respect given to the functional leader may be the key factor, as may the nature of the reporting lines.

Sharing knowledge across tribal boundaries

Managers and employees, especially those who find playing 'political games' against their nature, often lament the realities as they see people looking after themselves and their domains at the expense of the greater good. Some academic writers also seem to postulate their organisational theories as if the motivation of all members of an organisation were pure, and management has just failed to harness their altruism. The question for the Learning Organisation is how to recognise where the sources of conflict and non-co-operation are, and yet devise mechanisms that will overcome and work around them. This is not going to be achieved by decree (though constant messages and examples from leaders will help) but by setting up win-win environments.

Henry Mintzberg lists 13 political games under the headings:

- designed to resist authority
- designed to counter resistance
- designed to build power bases
- designed to defeat rivals
- designed to change the organisation

Readers are referred also to the study of 'defensive mechanisms' by Chris Argyris (*On Organisational Learning*); and *Understanding Organisations* by Charles Handy.

This is a fascinating area, but we must focus on some of the answers rather than the analysis of the problems. How do Learning Organisations differentiate themselves by overcoming some of the forces arrayed against them?

Storing knowledge and making it available

The sum of the knowledge and experience accumulated by everyone in the organisation over the years is potentially vast. What do we do with it all? Do we observe people investigating things that we know have already been done before? Do we clear out cupboards and find long-forgotten reports on subjects of current relevance? Surely it would be a simple thing to create a database of the learning in the organisation? Did we use to have a company library, which was closed follwing a round of cost-cutting?

We are very much up against the impatience of human nature here. The inherent forces against the perfectly logical step of 'asking first' are seen in such comments as:

- 'I know what to do, and I want to do it my way.'
- 'My predecessor/that department/those people over there made a real mess of things; there is nothing to learn from them.'
- 'This is a completely new situation.'
- 'I haven't time to do research; what we want is action around here.'

Impatience, pressure from above, personal pride – all get in the way. But is it not a good thing for people to make mistakes, so long as they learn from them? Of course – *but can the organisation afford to go on making the same mistakes over and over*?

We discuss the uses of information technology in assisting the Learning Organisation in Chapter 5. But the question here is one of cultural values. Very powerful tools are available, yet success is more to do with human failure than lack of technology. Some cultural values will help a lot – openness of communication, 'freedom of speech', respect for one another, 'humility' – although these cannot be forced. They need to be role-modelled by senior and influential people. A personnel director joined a blue-chip company, and was told on the first day, 'Just remember there is no such thing as a throw-away line here, especially from newcomers!' He watched his words carefully during his years of survival there.

To be effective, we need two basic disciplines to take place:

- Before embarking on a new line of enquiry, people must find out what is already known both within the organisation and outside it.

- Knowledge acquired must be logged or referenced in the organisation's database.

It is the second of these disciplines that is difficult to enforce; the 'what's in it for me?' syndrome encourages the first one but discourages the second.

The types of knowledge we would expect to see accessible would include:

- *results of research, reports, experiments, conclusions; uses of consultants or other suppliers.* At Procter & Gamble in the early 1970s it was an accepted rule in the manufacturing and logistics operation that, while experimentation was actually encouraged, nothing could be initiated without reference to the library of experiments, which was copied manually around the world. Likewise every experiment had eventually to be written up on just one page and then be put into the library.
- *manuals of procedures and processes.* It is surprising how many processes are reinvented by organisations. Many of course need deliberate reinvention and customisation from time to time, but here we are talking about those being designed because earlier work is lost, inaccessible or available but not accessed for various reasons. In a strongly devolved structure this risk is much greater, and organisations today are rediscovering corporate synergy as they look at what can be sensibly 'shared'.
- *case notes of particular applications and problems solved that form precedents.* Many problems are new, but as many are not. Where difficult judgements have to be made, do we have access to the thinking that has been applied before? Lawyers are the people to learn from in this regard!
- *summaries (and locations of full reports) on proceedings of conferences and seminars.* One or several days may be devoted to the sharing of knowledge between delegates. Afterwards, do the relevant parts of such conferences and

seminars get logged in a way that makes them available to all?

- *data concerning governments, countries, competition, other organisations; general reference material – either internal or external.* One is constantly amazed at the time spent by people searching for basic reference material. If they are lucky they get pointed in the direction of someone who knows where to find the data. How much simpler to make it available to all through a data reference sharing process!
- *information on sharing networks.* In a Learning Organisation, networks appear and subside for the purpose of sharing information and ideas. People need to know about them so that they can join in as appropriate. We discuss this further in Chapter 5.
- *'continuous improvement' initiatives and successes.* Ideas that have been successful in yielding improvements in service, quality or productivity need to be circulated for the good of all. Looking back again to Procter and Gamble, they had posts called 'methods co-ordinators'. There were full-time jobs in encouraging continuous improvement, assessing benefits, and writing up successes for world-wide circulation, as well as ideas originating from other sites that were circulated monthly.
- *active projects and their membership in the organisation.* An accessible record of ongoing major or critical projects – be they research, productivity-oriented, problem-solving or whatever – will help people not to duplicate effort, as well as help the work done to be adequately shared.
- *individuals within or without the organisation who have 'been there before' and have special knowledge of a situation or the people relevant to it.* Knowing people and situations, how they reacted previously, the background to the organisation chart, is a volume of valuable accumulated wisdom that may not be written down. It is strange how sometimes the holders of such knowledge are not asked for their opinions, for all kinds of political reasons. As they see unnecessary mistakes being made they wring their hands like the man in our

Preface, asking, 'Will people in this organisation never learn?' Of course they *are* learning from their mistakes, but is this a competitive way to do it?

Are there models that we can emulate? In *Liberation Management* Tom Peters devotes four chapters to what he calls 'knowledge management structures' – his name for a Learning Organisation. He advocates 'destroying Headquarters as a residence of expertise, and [replacing] it with smart accessible networks'. Peters describes in detail the workings of powerful sharing networks and databases at McKinsey's, the management consultancy, and the philosophy that every client project must be seen as a learning opportunity *for the firm*. We make the following observations about the McKinsey approach:

- Success has been driven by a 'director of knowledge management'.
- The rationale for, and the importance of, the approach were strongly marketed internally.
- 'Knowledge management capability' has been built into selection criteria for jobs.
- There are incentives to participate.
- A small number of customer-conscious, helpful consultants run the support systems.

Achieving the level of success that McKinsey's have (where it is easy to sell the concept of knowledge-sharing) is no simple task.   There will be objections such as:

- security
- editing power/filtration
- costs
- dividing lines on requirements – what is worth sharing?
- time needed to co-operate.

These are all problems that most firms solve in relation to data concerning customers. We need serious database and network management skills, and *disciplines*. The question is: if you considered your firm as a rival to McKinsey's, would you be worried if you foiund that you did not have the same capability?

⚡ **POWERPOINT**

Does your organisation have a 'knowledge management' team, with a respected and effective director?

Does every individual know that he or she is expected to access a library of data and experiences owned by the organisation?

Is a process established throughout your organisation for people to share their learning through contributing to an appropriate library or database?

Pointers for action

Every organisation has a unique culture, and it needs to be well understood and worked *with* if we want to achieve change. The Learning Organisation affects everyone from top to bottom. If we want to realise its power, we need to:

- examine the values that we have and ensure that they explicitly support continuous learning; if not, consider re-setting them
- study the language that is used in the organisation and if necessary make changes that reinforce the message of learning in titles, documents and processes
- help leaders understand role-model behaviours, and to assess themselves on a regular basis
- ensure that allocations of time and money reflect the importance of learning
- understand the forces of tribalism and boundaries in the organisation and study all the types of knowledge and experience that should be shared across them

- ensure that mechanisms for this sharing are embedded in the way things are done and in the norms of behaviour.

These are not actions that can be completed in just a few weeks. They require understanding of their importance and time to implement them through a managed change programme. In the end, the culture of an organisation determines what can be achieved.

4

The Power of Supportive Processes for People Management

The 'system' – help or hindrance?

The actual interface between individuals and their organisation consists of more than their interaction with another set of individuals. They are also embraced by the more or less formalised processes of administration, usually designed and maintained by finance or personnel departments. The majority of these systems were traditionally designed on the basis that:

- Employees need to be controlled.
- Managers are the agents of control.
- Personnel and finance departments ensure that managers control consistently.

Especially in large organisations, and historically in the public sector in particular, these systems effectively reward 'game-playing' by managers and other employees alike, and discourage risk-taking, experimentation, and innovation. The relationship between 'systemisation' and 'innovation' is an interesting cultural study. The startlingly experimental companies of Silicon Valley in California are known for their informality and rejection of 'straight-jacket' systems. In a country such as Italy, where systems are not always adhered to, a national characteristic flair and innovation. The Learning Organisation needs empowered people who are *supported* in their continuous learning by the systems, rather than being *restrained*. A good example is whether the expense claim system is elaborately controlled with numerous allowances and pre-authorisations (which may encourage the wrong sort of creativity) or is just a set of guidelines within which employees are trusted to claim the actual expenditure they have felt necessary to do their job. Human resource systems need to be looked at very closely in their support of the Learning Organisation.

Employees and managers, sometimes to quite high levels, love to blame the 'system'. 'The company will never allow it', 'this company doesn't encourage that kind of thing' are statements frequently heard. They may be reflections of the culture, or of the systems, or of individuals who control the systems, but they are used as defences and boundaries to job space. This can be a self-imposed ceiling on initiative.

Most of them are not plastered ceilings, but layers of cloud. They often *look like* impenetrable layers, but the truth is that the hassle of fighting through them is not seen to be worth the effort. 'Some you can win, some you can't – so let's concentrate on the winners'.

In the Learning Organisation, the cloud layers are such that glimpses of blue sky can be seen. Nothing is impenetrable because it is understood that open dialogue is desirable, that questioning of practices and accepted wisdom is important. The impersonal and omnipotent 'company' has disappeared.

To release the full potential power of learning we have to ask a number of questions of all our policies, processes and procedures. For example, is the time-hallowed job description a way of encouraging learning beyond the boundaries? Does it make sense for an appraisal system to assume that a *manager* owns all the data on a person's performance, and that it is their exclusive role to define and authorise training? Does the approach to pay and rewards actively encourage continuous learning, or quite different motivations?

Is there still a place for 'systems', if we can use that generic word? Certainly. We would argue all organisations need a framework within which people can be flexible. It should specifically *encourage* and *reinforce* the behaviours that we believe are needed. Systems are in fact much more powerful than value statements – they are the practical application of those values. They must reinforce the messages, clearly and unambiguously.

In this chapter we will look at the following processes which are essential to releasing the power of the Learning Organisation:

- performance management and feedback
- defining learning plans
- role descriptions
- selection for roles
- induction
- resource management
- career management
- monetary rewards
- non-monetary rewards
- opinion surveys
- skills planning.

The system for 'how am I doing?'

More must have been written on 'performance appraisals' than on any other process of people management. Culturally, it seems a particularly Anglo-American obsession to have something that is rigorously systematic. Southern Europeans, for example, are more comfortable feeding back feelings about strengths and weaknesses; most Asians prefer to avoid negatives and concentrate on strengths, leaving weaknesses to be inferred.

Performance-based pay, especially in the UK (including the public sector), has meant that even in the mid-1990s systems are being introduced for the first time. Some of these are quite innovative, such as that from Hertfordshire County Council described here.

The accepted wisdom is that systems should be built around the setting of individual, measurable objectives that can be factually assessed at the end of a period, normally a year. The assessment of performance follows a hierarchical framework, and is reviewed in a private discussion between a manager and his or her subordinate. How often is the cry heard, 'she can't

---

HERTFORDSHIRE COUNTY COUNCIL

Appraisal of Teachers and Head-teachers

Teachers

- The appraisal defines the benefits to the teacher, the pupils, the school, and the education authority.
- No appraiser should be responsible for more than four appraisees; if there are more than four under one head, a separate appraiser such as a colleague, head, or deputy head may be requested to assist.
- Training is required for all appraisers *and* appraisees.
- A continuous cycle runs over two years for each appraisal.
- Self-appraisal is encouraged.
- Defined classroom observation and the total job (including non-teaching duties) are included.
- Outputs include targets for action, training and development.

Head-teachers

- Head-teachers are appraised by an area adviser *and* a consultant head-teacher in a similar field of work.
- The appraisal includes data relating to the work of the school in the community, the school development plan, interviews with governors and parent representatives, and officers of the education authority.
- Data is collected over a whole term.
- The appraisal dialogue is held with both appraisers present.
- A review meeting takes place between all parties after one year.

---

be disturbed at the moment, she is doing an appraisal' – and the caller recognises the sanctity of such a discussion. Much emphasis has been placed on the accuracy of performance evaluation, so that a clear connection can be made to the pay reward in the mind of the person under appraisal. Systems vary in the weighting they give to *results achieved* (some would say this is all that matters in the end) and *the application of competence in achieving the results* (strengths and weaknesses, to use more traditional terms). The outcomes are typically a performance rating or summary – and countless hours have been spent by people in personnel functions agonising over definitions of particular ratings.

In a Learning Organisation, performance feedback is clearly of fundamental importance in understanding what and how we can improve through learning activities. Some challenges to the traditions are needed, however. For example:

- *Does it make sense to say that the manager – however junior or inexperienced – is the best person both to observe and feed back data on performance? Does not he or she see only a part of the whole, which itself may be a filtered part anyway?* The assumption here is that the manager has not only a unique and comprehensive knowledge of the person's performance, but is the best person to communicate it. This is a big assumption. There are many inherent problems here, such as the dissatisfaction that comes from being rated on a few very visible measures with little or no account being taken of the difficulties encountered or overcome to achieve the results – or of the imbalance often found in assessments biased towards recent history or just one or two incidents. Despite training in feedback skills, managers still vary over a wide spectrum in their ability to give good feedback to their people, and even more so in their ability to work towards good learning objectives and appropriate solutions.

  The manager is primarily concerned about results, and is likely to see the performance of an individual in terms of the contribution to those he or she regards as the most important. Naturally this is a key area, but the 'why and how' of achievement may lie in the way that peer, subordinate or customer relationships are managed (for example). It is often the case in today's de-layered organisations that a manager has very little time to spend with each individual, and so relies on them to get on with their work largely unsupervised. Of course, the theory of empowered de-layered organisations is that the manager's prime role is as 'coach'. Though this is occasionally seen at the very top of organisations, life is not always like that down below in the engine-rooms, where de-layering may just have meant more work all round for everybody who is left!

- *What is the value in pursuing great degrees of accuracy in performance evaluation – other than to have a fair reward if it is based on performance elements – when the real benefit is going to be the learning from that performance?* Well-managed organisations go to great lengths to define and measure performance. This has its place in every part of the enterprise. Reviews of performance should be held regularly, certainly not just annually in this fast-changing world. 'School-report'-type data on individual performance may lead us to some pay or bonus decisions, but our real objective is to get behind the performance results and to work out how improvements in knowledge, skills, attitudes and experience will yield even better results.
- *Why should this be a hierarchically owned process, where the very term 'appraisee' implies the person is the object rather than the subject? Surely the ownership should be with the individual, the person who will primarily gain from the process?* This is the heart of an empowered culture: that I as an employee have prime ownership for my performance, its improvement, my development and my career. Not exclusively so, but more than any other. It is one of the secrets of power in a Learning Organisation – mobilised, motivated, individual ownership of constant improvement and development.
- *What is the role of the personnel department? Is it to check that the paper system is working and appraisals have all been done on time and are neatly filed? Is it to help organise some of the agreed training courses? Or is it to add real consultancy value to the learning process?* The role of policeman needs to be replaced by one of adding value to the process. Of course the resources do not exist in today's organisations either in quality or quantity to have consultants for every manager-individual relationship. But not everyone needs consultant help every year, especially if we have instituted some personal ownership of learning and have supplied resources that each person can access.

We must conclude that a more holistic view of the objectives of

Figure 4.1
The performance and development loop

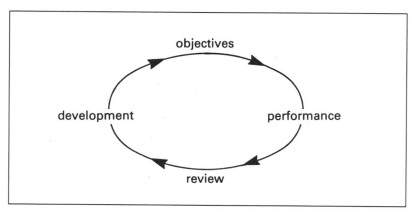

appraisal systems might lead to more flexible approaches. We need to reconsider the whole process of managing the performance and development loop (see Figure 4.1).

We should answer the following questions, to which there may be different answers in different cases, and then set up a system that is sufficiently flexible to deal with the variety of needs:

- Are we interested in setting performance objectives for the individual, a team to which they may belong, or a combination of both?
- If learning is our prime aim, both for improving current role performance and towards preparation for the future, then who has an input to make, and against which competency categories, in providing feedback on performance?
- How is data best collected and analysed so that it can be turned into helpful feedback?
- Who should be involved in defining the learning needs for an individual?
- Who should be involved in helping the individual to plan for longer-term career growth?

Figure 4.2
Multi-input feedback

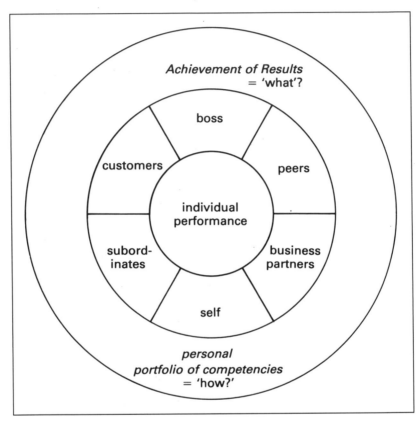

Multi-input appraisal

The idea of 'multi-input' (or even '360°') appraisal is to recognise that there are different perspectives on performance, and that some interfaces are better able to feed back on certain aspects than others. This may be applied to the performance of a team or an individual, but more commonly the latter. The management of this feedback process has many options. Perceptions from different sources enable the subject of the appraisal to compare their personal perception of skills and abilities with the perception of others.

It makes sense for the individual to manage the setting of his or her own objectives by referring to the demands of the role held (assuming they are quite clear about the business context which it occupies); and personally to manage the feedback and ensure the right degree of help on the development planning. That is, *own the entire process.*

The task of co-ordinating opinions may be done by the manager, by a supporting HR consultant, or by the individual. Perhaps the most developed approach is where individuals initiate feedback themselves, analyse it, and bring it to the appraisal discussion with the manager as an input. We have tried this ourselves to great benefit. Or a co-ordinated, resourced approach may be used, affecting a group of participants. The data collection may take the following forms:

- *open questions such as 'what do you think X has done particularly well?' and 'what do you think X should focus on for improvement?'* These are very general and free-form. They may elicit unhelpful generalisations or really specific pointers that might not have emerged from a questionnaire approach. However, if backed up by one-to-one discussions with contributors they can be extremely valuable.
- *questionnaires related to specific aspects of performance and behaviour, using a spectrum of 'high' to 'low' rating, with or without free comments added.* These may be individualised to cover areas of concern or interest to the person. There is of course the risk of bias towards 'what one would like to hear', but it does give the opportunity to add aspects of an individual's unique contribution.
- *ratings on a defined competency profile relevant to the role.* Some organisations have defined competency profiles for roles, encouraged in the UK by various national bodies who have attempted to do this across a wide spectrum. As we discuss under 'rewards' (see pages 101–6), such profiles are

likely to grow in order to support competency-based pay systems. Some consultancies, such as Savile and Holdsworth, are developing comprehensive assessment questionnaires for general use.

The systematic, thorough approach has its appeal; however, in practice real value can come from being less formalised and more open-ended.

There are a couple of issues to be considered if the process is to be made the norm. First, there is a level of openness and readiness needed to accept this breadth and depth of feedback. This is dependent on the maturity of both the organisation and the individual. Second, there is a question of anonymity – some approaches are completely open, others have feedback averaged in the interests of not identifying individual contributors and therefore eliciting greater honesty. As personal experimenters with this approach, we would unhesitatingly recommend the maximum of openness and minimum of anonymity in order to gain the greatest benefit. Indeed, we have received great value from honest feedback from various sources.

Multi-input feedback is particularly appropriate for people managers, as staff are in frequent contact with their manager and observe or experience a large number of performance-relevant behaviours. IBM has used their annual opinion survey for many years to provide feedback on individual managers and their styles for this purpose.

Many organisations have several years' experience now of such feedback systems. In a report by the UK organisation Incomes Data Services in May 1994, the retail company W.H. Smith was reported as having decided to formalise upward appraisal to all its 650 managers after four years' experimentation with senior managers. A standard questionnaire with 32 attributes is used, and analysis is by an independent source. Other organisations well advanced in this practice are Rank Xerox, Du Pont and American Express – the latter making it a voluntary decision on the part of managers. Self-appraisal is generally encouraged, but this leads only to a more mutual one-to-one dialogue between a manager and his or her sub-ordinate.

Design considerations

In considering a multi-input feedback approach, the following are some of the questions that might be asked:

- Is the approach to be voluntary or compulsory?
- Is it to be used for management only, or everyone?
- Is the main purpose for development or performance evaluation?
- Will the input data be confidential or open?
- Will the process be internally or externally facilitated?
- Is the subject to be an individual or a team?
- Will the data be collected manually or electronically?
- Who will analyse the data?
- Will the subject manage the feedback personally or look for other support?
- Will the feedback be shared amongst contributors?

Psychologists worry about reliability and validity in any questionnaire-oriented exercise. In this case there seems to be a simple question to ask: 'was the feedback more or less helpful in understanding the drivers of performance and the indicators for needed development? It is going to be unusual, we feel, for the answer to be negative. We should note that the process of *averaging scores* can become quite *un*helpful, as it is in the detail and the extremes that the value of feedback is found.

We feel that the process of feedback is a foundation for the Learning Organisation, and that whoever seeks that ideal needs to examine carefully the most appropriate systems of feedback.

Example

John was a strong manager. In his appraisal by his boss he was complimented on his ability to show clear direction to his people. Yet his team all experienced in their own right, told him in their own ways that they felt his influence was diminished by the forcefulness of his opinions, and that he would obtain more commitment by listening to their perspectives and allowing a team consensus on the direction to emerge. He felt able to discuss with each of them observed examples that had led them to conclude what they did. Without this added dimension of feedback John's behaviour would have continued to be reinforced by his boss.

 POWERPOINT

Is the process for evaluating and discussing performance one that encourages the input of data from all relevant sources to help with personal development?

Do the majority of managers and staff feel that the culture supports *open* feedback?

Is the primary ownership of feedback with the individual?

Is there a flexibility of choice in the approach to performance feedback, depending on individual preference and readiness?

Making a learning plan

In Chapter 3 we discussed why ownership of individual learning *by* the individual is important for the Learning Organisation; in Chapter 8 we discuss how to extract the full benefits from the range of learning opportunities. We could argue that there is no need to specify a process, but if we are going to have one for performance feedback then it must feed automatically into a learning plan. Such plans are a foundation of continuous learning.

Again, the tradition has been to put the onus on the manager to complete various forms, or parts of them, which specify the 'development actions' for the coming year. All too frequently this is in the form of training courses from the company catalogue or elsewhere, when there is a wealth of different and action-orientated learning opportunities available. The assumption that the manager should be regarded as solely accountable, and is knowledgeable and skilled in helping an individual define their learning needs, must be questioned. On the one hand organisations have insisted that it is a prime managerial task to develop one's staff, and on the other they lament how little time and effort managers spend on it. It is time not to deny such a role, but to rebalance this process.

Though we do want to see all managers having the skills of coaching, we want the skill of defining learning needs and choosing good and relevant solutions to be a shared expertise. The reality is that relatively few managers today find the time and intellectual energy to do this well. It is probably the case that *a majority of people* are being appraised by relatively junior managers who are unlikely to know all the opportunities offered by the organisation. Likewise, team leaders or junior managers may have little experience of helping others learn. We certainly want to see their skills develop, but should not place a requirement on them which is unreasonable and one which they cannot fulfil.

The learning plan should be the main output from the review of performance. Thus we elicit strengths to be reinforced, weaknesses to be overcome, attitudes to be changed, and experience that is needed. *It is not a training plan*. It requires the setting of measurable learning objectives, the choice of a learning solution, and milestones for measuring progress.

Some consultant help, either live or electronic, is bound to be beneficial where available. We would like to see 'learning consultants' available to all, based on Figure 3.1, able to advise the definition of objectives and the choice of learning routes.

Figure 4.3
Personal learning plan

NAME:	PERIOD:		
LEARNING NEEDS	ACTION CHOSEN	RESP	WHEN BY
KNOWLEDGE:			
SKILL:			
ATTITUDES:			
EXPERIENCE:			
Owned by: Employee: Assisted by: Manager: Unit HR consultant:	Last updated:		

Given that this is likely to be a scarce resource, 'Learning Options Guides' should be made available to everyone in the organisation. This concept is expanded on pages 123–4 and 140–1.

The learning plan should be based on:

- enhancing the capability to do the current role better, and maybe expand it
- areas of learning that will facilitate the chosen career/ personal growth plan (where appropriate).

We recommend that it is split into *knowledge, skills, attitudes* and *experience*, and may look something like Figure 4.3.

A learning plan is not a once-a-year affair. There is a natural opportunity to reset the plan at the time of a performance feedback or career-planning review, but many 'learning steps' may merit review as frequently as once a month. Since a number of the chosen solutions will be work-oriented, these plans should be live and dynamic and regularly referred to.

⚡ POWERPOINT

Do individuals at all levels have a learning plan that they personally own, covering knowledge, skills, attitudes, and experience?

Do such plans specify learning objectives and utilise a range of learning solutions to achieve them?

Are they both reviewed and renewed regularly?

Describing roles

We are deliberately using the word 'roles' rather than 'jobs'. The concept of a fixed 'job description' does not fit in with an empowered Learning Organisation where we want to give individuals space to expand and learn in response to a changing environment, and to contribute more effectively to the organisation's goals. In a moving, flexible organisation such fixed descriptions fall quickly out of date.

The idea is not, however, that people can pick and choose their own role descriptions as they wish, because that would never provide effective functioning of the organisation. People, even within defined descriptions, have a tendency to spend their discretionary time on what interests them most, which does not necessarily lead to a balanced fulfilment of the role. But they may well want to change or broaden those descriptions as they see opportunities for learning, and obtain agreement to do so. We could quote many personal examples when we have sought

Figure 4.4
Growth of capability

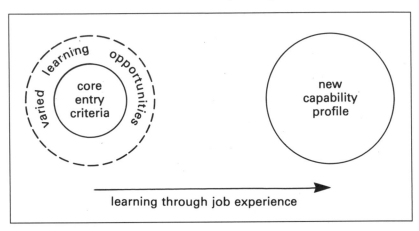

expanded or new responsibilities; the original role is mastered in time, and there is some free space to be filled.

Role descriptions should be entirely in terms of *account-abilities*. We do not want to specify *how* a role should be carried out; only what it is, and what the expected performance measures are. It is then helpful to specify the *capabilities* needed to do the role, specified in terms of *knowledge, skills, attitudes* and *experience*. This helps us not only to choose people suitable for the role, but also to assess the performance.

We need to look at the specification for roles in two parts, as depicted in Figure 4.4. The core entry criteria define the minimum levels of knowledge, skills, attitudes and experience necessary for the role. The entire role is defined by these *plus* the learning opportunities that the role offers as the learning curve proceeds. Typically these would describe the opportunities to enhance capability in the four areas, and they will change and expand depending on the passage of time. After going through this learning experience the individual then has a larger profile to match against the entry requirements for the next role which, if not 'bigger' in traditional terms, will certainly be broader.

POWERPOINT

Do all roles in the organisation have a set of specified account-abilities rather than series of tasks?

Does each role have a profile of knowledge, skills, attitudes and experience appropriate to it, split clearly into entry criteria and learning opportunities?

Selecting for roles

Since the prime means of learning for personal development at our disposal lies in work itself, the way in which we utilise roles in organisations and give people new opportunities is very important.

The basis of selection for posts has been to find the person most suited for the job in terms of their *current readiness*. Selectors look for the person who will have the fastest learning curve – not because he or she may be fast learners but because they will have the least to learn and be of maximum use as quickly as possible. Of course, there is also the tendency to choose the person who 'we know will fit in' on the basis of past associations.

Although one could reasonably argue that this approach makes sense when bringing new people into the organisation for the first time, a Learning Organisation recognises that this is not efficient in the development of people within the organisation. We want to build up a culture of progression through learning, and need a framework for this to take place. Thus a person progresses through the organisation as in Figure 4.5.

Available roles should be matched against the 'experience' part of individual learning plans wherever possible. Those who own their personal plans should be able to go to a resource centre, where details of the competencies required of different roles or job families can be made available. People can then

Figure 4.5
Personal growth curve

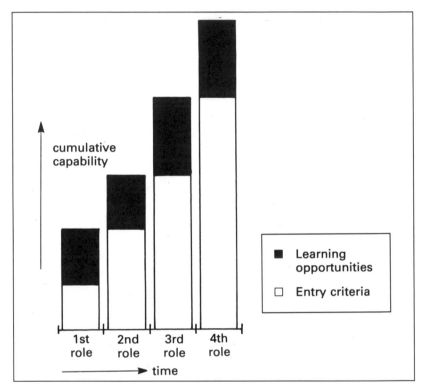

plot the progression that will most enhance their personal portfolio in the desired direction. There will be occasions when the organisation wants to invervene and help; it is a simplification to say, as some do today, that 'careers are now solely the responsibility of individuals'. We shall pick this up again on page 98.

This way of using roles is a significant change in thinking and not easy to embrace in fast-moving, expedient organisations. To accept that the basis of selection might be oriented towards learning rather than immediate results will sound Utopian and impractical. And yet so many people acknowledge as they look back on their personal learning odyssey the occasions when someone took a risk, gave them a chance – when they were *not* fully equipped for the task at the time. This is the essence of personal learning.

 **POWERPOINT**

Is a key aspect of selection for posts the matching of the core criteria with the experience requirements from individual learning plans?

Efficient induction

Induction is a process that is often neglected in organisations, especially for internal moves. People may be armed with a timetable of people to see, but they are expected to guess what they need to learn. We discussed in Chapter 1 the cost of poor learning curves. How can we make induction more effective?

A real and thorough introduction to where the learning material is – whether in people or documents – and then practical learning assignments to ensure appropriate analysis and synthesis of the information are what is needed. It requires some effort in preparation, but is both appreciated and effective. Here is a format learnt 25 years ago at Procter and Gamble, who followed this practice systematically.

Well-constructed, this format helps the individual to understand quickly the issues surrounding the job; know where to look for things subsequently; and have already thought through some of the challenges ahead. The manager guides and coaches the person through this period, reviewing progress from time to time – even though managing the assignments is self-directed. This induction needs to be scheduled as a *full-time* occupation and not be confused with getting started in the job at the same time. (This is not always possible, but should always be aimed for.)

INDUCTION PROGRAMMES

1. Contents
2. Welcome; profile of the job and its importance
3. Accountabilities
4. Timetable (approximate) for the induction
5. Sections covering each area of the job and specifying:
   • Learning Objectives
   – what the induction should enable the person to know or do
   • References
   – people or written material
   • Learning Assignments
   – specific self-directed assignments, for example to meet people and discuss things; to study reference material; to analyse and synthesise information; to collect data; to formulate opinions on something
   • Check-questions
   – to self-test on the depth of knowedge attained
6. Objectives for the next period

The same concepts should apply to new *teams* as well as individuals. So much productivity and effectiveness are lost when reorganisations occur because the new incumbents do not have the patience or discipline to go through some systematic learning. It should be a built-in requirement that all *outgoing* role-holders prepare an induction programme for their successor(s), referencing where all the knowledge in the organisation is to be found, and that all *incoming* role-holders start with the disciplines of picking up the knowedge already in the role or organisation.

 **POWERPOINT**

Do new recruits and job changers have professional, individualised induction programmes that work from their learning needs?

Is the same done where feasible for new teams?

Resource management

Organisations of the future will require greater flexibility in resource management. We will have far fewer people with 'permanent' contracts, or in today's sense 'full employees'. The determination of the 'core' skills will be a critical human resources decision, and will clearly include:

- *those key professional and technical skills* that provide distinctive competitive advantage. The dividing line between knowledge and skills that are uniquely valuable to the particular organisation, and those that anyone could sub-contract for, is a key decision.
- *a management capability* that understands the organisation and feels committed to its success. These managers provide leadership, determine direction and provide a sense of common cause for all contributors. Many of them will have built the history and culture of the organisation and hold the 'map' of how things work.

The key here is the need for *continuity*.

Charles Handy quotes the formula:

> ½ the number of people at **2** times the salary producing **3** times the added value.

This group forms one leaf of Handy's 'Shamrock Organisation', the other two being 'contractual partners' and 'temporary hired help'. Another way to describe the categories is in terms of 'inner-core', 'outer-core' and 'peripheral' workers. The skills infrastructure that exists on individual or agency contracting will become more diverse, richer and more sophisticated. It will include managers, all kinds of specialists traditionally seen as 'organisation people', and will particularly favour women owing to the flexibility inherent in such working styles. Powerful niche agencies will develop to assist the market in chosen skills, and these may themselves invest in the continuous learning of their members.

In the USA one in three workers is 'contingent', and such are expected to outnumber traditional employees by the year 2000. A study by NatWest Bank in 1993 reported that three times as many part-time jobs would be created for every full-time one that was lost, and that in the UK around 175,000 full-time jobs would disappear each year.

The distinction between 'insiders' and 'outsiders' has been quite clear in the past and few companies have worked through a new relationship. Yet the future must lie in creating a shared sense of purpose for the *partnership of resources*. How does this relate to a Learning Organisation? The *framework* of rewards and development must be different. We need mechanisms to learn from and to encourage learning *in all our partners*. So in ICL, for example, the learning department employs both full-time employees and 'associates'. The latter have specialist skills and are used as needed, perhaps for 10–30 weeks a year. The processes for sharing of knowledge across the department treat them as equals; their continuous learning is just as much a concern as that of their full-time colleagues.

On the one hand, it may mean we have partners with niche agencies who are sources of particular knowledge, skills and experience – continuously learning organisations in their own right, who add synergistically to our own. On the other, we may actively encourage and contribute to their learning, to our mutual benefit.

Recruitment policy

Mills and Friesen point out the importance of continuous learning through acquiring individuals and absorbing what they bring in terms of skills and experience. It is a way of renewal. *There is never a case for a recruitment ban in organisations, and especially not of new graduates.* When times are hard, and especially when downsizing is taking place, management likes to impose recruitment and graduate-hire freezes. This is done with the objective of helping this year's results by minimising costs. A Learning Organisation recognises the need to have a competitive cost-base, but it must also have competitive skills enhancement and innovation. So it learns to balance the flows in and out, and would never cut off the inflow of new blood. It should rejoice when it sees its competitors freezing training expenditure and hiring, knowing that puts them at a disadvantage.

Not all organisations believe in graduate recruitment and training for themselves. We believe, however, that the opportunity to harness the enthusiasm of young people towards the objectives of your organisation, to link them with your culture, and to give them a sense of mutual benefit is of real competitive value. Of course many young people deliberately want the experience of several employers, but few actually leave when they are well motivated.

Likewise it is recommended to have a *policy* regarding the balance of internal and external recruitment. Companies like IBM who never recruited externally above a certain level have had radically to rethink as they came to terms with their inability to manage change. As late as 1990, no one would have dreamed that a CEO who had never been in the IT industry would take the helm at IBM. The best way to learn from best practice is to hire the people who know how to implement it, as many a smaller company has learnt to their advantage.

A Learning Organisation that is organised in teams and has generally gone 'beyond hierarchy' in its thinking might adopt a team-based approach to hiring decisions. Thus the view of the team members as to the added value of the new member may well be the nub of the decision-making process.

 **POWERPOINT**

Do you have a clear definition of the skills and roles that should be core resources in order to give your organisation unique competitive advantage?

> Do you have partnership resources that identify and share in your organisation's success?
>
> Do you help your part-time resources with their own continual learning?
>
> Does your organisation have a continuing strategy for acquiring new people, both in terms of fresh young people, and through deliberate infeed of new ideas at all levels?

Career management processes

Career management in most organisations has been built on the basis of hierarchical progression, with visible signs of status as one progresses upwards. Large organisations have had sophisticated frameworks and individuals can be forgiven for expecting a 'job for life', as they have been part of a structure which is based on such an assumption.

We can look at available career management processes as follows:

Individual career-planning processes	Joint career-planning processes	Organisational processes
– Occupational choice assessment/ counselling	– Appraisal and development reviews	– Appointment processes
– Career-planning workshops	– Potential assessment centres	– Career structures
– Self-development plans/activities	– Career guidance/ development centres	– High-flyer schemes
– Use of career resource centres	– Mentoring	– Succession/ pool-planning
– Careers seminars	– Career planning	
– Personal competency profiling	– Outplacement	– Creating opportunities for experience
– Writing CVs and 'personal growth profiles'	– Career breaks and alternative methods of employment	– Manpower planning

There is certainly an emphasis today on shifting from the right of the table to the left, and on making data and tools available to individuals to enable them to take greater charge of their own careers. There is a need for a very fundamental move in the understanding of the word 'careers'. The move has to be:

from	to
• thinking 'careers'	• thinking 'increasing personal value'
• rewards based on promotion to my level of (in)competence	• rewards based on my accumulated and applied learning
• working in a secure environment	• working in a flexible/ uncertain environment
• being limited by life-balancing decisions	• being unlimited, with different life-balancing decisions

This shift is quite compatible with the Learning Organisation. It is being driven by structural de-layering and reduced reliance on permanent employee contracts – changes that are fundamentally economic and cost-led rather than learning-investment led. It means giving more attention to profiling roles along the lines of Figure 4.3 so that individuals can see where they can make bridges. A career framework built on hierarchical steps upwards, which causes people to make moves for reasons that have nothing to do with their continued learning, has always been a problem to management developers. The traditional job evaluation schemes were based on job size and position in the hierarchy, and did not value the learning opportunities inherent in the role. Thus, for example, a richly loaded learning opportunity in an Eastern European operation might be of a lowly grade due to its low level of current business turnover – and therefore avoided by the ambitious. In a Learning Organisation such positions constitute the prizes to be sought.

We need a career framework that visibly encourages and rewards increased personal value. Many organisations have technical and professional career structures linked to defined competencies, and these provide a good base. Such structures describe stages of increasing capability to produce outputs or provide a service. Some examples are reproduced in Mayo's *Managing Careers*. If we can make these available to individuals – using software available which enables the matching of a personal capability template with specific roles – then those individuals can take prime responsibility for their career planning. They will identify the elements of knowledge, skills, attitudes and experience that they need for desired roles, and feed these into their personal learning plan.

Examples of career progression structures, or 'role families' as they are sometimes called, might be:

- technical
- customer-focused
- professional, support
- administration, clerical
- production, manual
- managerial.

In addition to the focus on skill levels, there needs to be some statement of expected outputs, and the impact on the business or customers. Length of time in position, age, or length of service should *not* be specified.

Certain types of career directions, notably those towards general management, require specific experience moves that are unlikely to occur without intervention by the organisation in some way. So a Learning Organisation is quite legitimately concerned with some planning of the growth of certain sections of its population. We would see these as:

- the senior executive group
- those likely to be the next entrants to the senior executive group
- young entrants in their first few years.

The disciplines of succession planning and career management still apply in a Learning Organisation as we seek to ensure that the necessary experiences are planned for at the right time. However, assessments of potential based on attaining *future levels or grades* may be inappropriate, and some new ways of describing future capability will be needed. One approach is to talk in terms of 'taking broader accountability' for leaders, and 'achieving levels of recognised expertise' for professional and technical contributors.

 POWERPOINT

Does your organistion have 'role families' which outline the core entry knowledge, skills, attitudes and experience requirements for stages of increased value?

Are they accessible to individuals for the purpose of their own career planning?

Are the systems used for succession planning and potential rating appropriate for the Learning Organisation you would like to have?

Monetary rewards

Traditional reward systems have been built on the basis of paying for *current job value* with adjustments based partly on market movements and partly on performance. In an organisation where one wants to encourage learning, flexibility, and teamwork, the traditional structures for rewards become unsatisfactory. Job evaluation processes focus on the internal relativities of positions, award more points for vertical rather than horizontal growth, and do not recognise the growth in job responsibilities that an individual may have more scope and freedom to develop. They encourage employees to compete with the system for more points, rather than thinking about how they could help the business to compete externally, maybe with fewer people and assets, and at the same time enhance their own value and net worth.

Salary systems based on a grade, fixed by a hierarchical position and static job description, cause people to make career decisions for reasons that do not promote continuous learning. (There is however much evidence that managers manipulate the system to ensure that people are actually paid according to how they perceive their market value.) Reward systems should:

- favour lateral growth rather than hierarchical promotions
- focus on accumulated capability and its application to outputs
- provide space and encouragement for roles to expand
- encourage leadership more than management
- encourage initiative, ie creativity and risk-taking related to the business
- focus on market value more than internal equitability.

We outlined in the previous section on career management the need for structures that specify the capabilities needed and the outputs expected. Just as employee learning results in movements up and sometimes across these structures, so employees' remuneration can be linked to the ability to fulfil a particular role. Some control is needed to ensure there is not rapid upwards progression based on the learning of new capabilities themselves; they must be capable of *being used* to produce results or a level of output that go along with the capability acquired. We would expect a gap between gaining new learning and reward, except in circumstances – such as a production department – where that learning has immediate application.

Towards a new pay strategy

We can look at a 'pay for value' approach as follows:

Role title	+ Entry criteria in knowledge, skills, attitudes, experience	+ Typical outputs	≫ Market-based salary range
stages in job family	specified for each stage	eg size of project, sales target, service level	flexed for cumulative previous experience

Employees manage their own development towards those capability criteria appropriate for a higher stage in the job family, and when the opportunity to provide that output arises their additional learning is rewarded. There are some types of job where 'stages' may legitimately be replaced with a 'continuum' – so people might expect smaller salary adjustments more frequently rather than step-wise promotions. It is probably to be recommended that increases arising from inflationary changes in market rates are reflected in the increases for learning rather than a separate 'cost of living' adjustment.

The traditional *consistency* that personnel departments have always encouraged must be questioned in a Learning Organisation. Different parts of the organisation may wish to adopt different positions in relation to the market value of the skills they employ.

The ability to change does depend very much upon the current pay environment within the organisation. If it is already formalised, expectations of both managers and employees may lead towards a relatively structured alternative. However, there are opportunities for systems that focus on guidelines and judgement rather than precision.

Positioning in a particular job family requires the following:

- a system to measure the core elements of the role, the capabilities needed for success and the outputs or account-abilities which impact on the business
- a system for managers to use that evaluates an employee's capabilities against the requirements and the results which he or she achieves.
- benchmarking ranges of capability against the external and internal pay markets.

There is a risk that such systems are as overengineered as previous job evaluation schemes were.

One of the dangers for an organisation is that time and effort are spent developing employees when they do not have the ability, or the organisation does not need the additional skills. Diagnostic tools to assess learning capability are important here.

Whither 'pay for performance'?

The need for high levels of performance for both individuals and (increasingly cross-functional) teams continues, although different ways of rewarding good performance may be needed. The popular performance pay systems of the 1980s may require a new look. An individual's performance is not the same every year, and is always dependent on the highly variable degree of difficulty encountered. One person's set of objectives may seem unreasonably easy or difficult to another. To link increases in basic salary to successful performance is therefore unnecessarily inflationary, and should probably be rewarded with specific lump sum bonus payments. These can be individual, team or a combination of both.

A suitable rewards structure for a Learning Organisation is described below.

Basic salary based on:
- job family
- market relativities
- accumulated individual capabilities.

Increases for:
- development and use of personal skills and abilities (subject to need and affordability)
- special market changes
- increased core-role responsibilities.

Variable pay based on:
- personal results
- team results (where appropriate)
- customer satisfaction.

Changing the pay structure is a fundamental cultural change, and probably the most powerful. The environment to achieve such a transition may take time to achieve. A number of tools are needed as well as fundamental cultural changes for it to succeed. The reality is that all of these changes will develop at different paces in different parts of the organisation, being very dependent on local leadership. The tools that will be helpful towards this new rewards regime will include:

- team evaluation (peer appraisal)
- multi-input appraisal
- customer appraisal
- ranking
- competency profiling.

Mills and Friesen, in discussing the cluster organisation of BP Engineering, describe two three-part scales used to evaluate the performance of engineers. They are:

1. Professional technical skills
   (i) *Versatility*: ability to apply skills outside the area currently being worked in
   (ii) *Productivity*: an output assessment
   (iii) *Technical competence*: applied level of technological knowledge and experience

2. Personal and people skills
   (i) *Consultancy skills*: persuading and influencing others
   (ii) *Client acceptability*: accepted and in demand from internal and possibly external worlds
   (iii) *Self-standing*: taking personal responsibility for work and learning without supervision

Pay is based on a scoring system – by cluster leaders through appropriate multi-input evaluations – and goes up as applied competence increases.

POWERPOINT

Does your organisation have a remuneration system that rewards continuous learning and its application rather than fixed jobs?

Does it have a clear view of what should be rewarded by base pay and what by variable bonus?

Non-monetary rewards

Just as important as monetary rewards in the sense of pay and bonuses are awards for successful learning or positive contributions to the Learning Organisation. These may take various forms. The most obvious is *accreditation*, traditionally given for significant course completion. Thus a nice certificate signed by a senior executive graces many an office wall with pride. Even though the recipient may not have learnt too much from the sessions on the course, we can be sure that the interaction with colleagues was of real value.

Another area is that of rewards for *ideas and innovation*. The old style 'suggestion scheme' will have been largely replaced by various schemes linked with total quality management initiatives. Awards may be certificates, prizes, badges, visits, dinners with senior people, or just being publicly honoured. Similar themes may be applied to customer satisfaction and responsiveness. Most important of all is to reward innovative products and services that will materially affect the organisation's business. Companies have a variety of schemes to do this, such as 'distinguished clubs', innovation awards, and special cups or plaques.

ICL has the following scheme for recognising special performance:

Excellence Scheme – ICL

- Bronze, Silver and Gold pins plus gifts of increasing value are awarded.
- Awards are for individual or team effort.
- Criteria for assessment:
  'Role model' plus four of the following:

Quality improvement	Exceeding expectations
Putting the customer first	Best practice
Meet promises and commitments	Waste reduction

- Anyone can nominate candidates for an award.
- Publicity and prestige accrue from the awards.

We would recommend award schemes for innovation in *learning* itself – for individuals or teams who have shown creativity in learning effectiveness – and also for parts of the organisation achieving advancement in the benchmarks of a Learning Organisation.

Perhaps the best reward in a Learning Organisation is the opportunity to have a special learning experience. Some examples might be:

- a trip to an interesting and unfamiliar part of the organisation

- an external course or seminar in a new or challenging environment
- selection for membership of a special project or task force
- selection for being a representative of the organisation externally
- being a 'shadow' of a senior executive for a period.

There is the opportunity for considerable creativity here, if the benefits of *experiential* learning are well understood.

In organisations with less opportunity for promotion, *expanded job responsibilities* may be a form of reward – with opportunities for new learning and increasing personal value.

 **POWERPOINT**

Does your organisation have award schemes recognising learning achievements that are valued by recipients and respected by colleagues?

Does your organisation have awards for innovation that are prestigious and valued?

Does your organisation use special learning experiences as part of the reward portfolio?

Checking where you are – using opinion surveys

One of the most helpful measures of progress in cultural change is to ask people what they feel and experience as reality. This gets away from the problem of 'being told what you want to hear', that even in the best Learning Organisations may still exist in upwards communication channels. It is a valuable process in *organisational learning* itself, provided the organisation listens and reacts to the results. We can use such surveys to check the effectiveness of feedback processes, the value of learning in various forms, views of pay systems, and so on. Typical questions might be:

- Do you feel you personally own a learning plan that meets your need for better job performance and career development?
- Do you feel that effort in learning new things is rewarded?
- Do you feel you have adequate opportunity for progression?
- Are you encouraged to share knowledge and experience with other departments?
- Do you feel you have ready access to the knowledge available in the company?

Such surveys need to be coupled with visible communication of the results and commitment to some improvement actions to retain credibility.

 **POWERPOINT**

Does your organisation utilise regular surveys of employee opinion that enable it to track cultural changes?

Does the survey include questions that support specific changes designed to achieve a better Learning Organisation?

Future skills planning

Skills planning needs to be carried out at different levels in the organisation in a cascaded way. At the strategic 'overview level' one is interested in the generic capability descriptions. At the operational business level, roles and numbers of people in those roles will be determined by the structural plan and by the desired productivity ratios. Thus you may need to achieve sales of £1 million, and want to achieve a ratio of an average £100,000 per sales head (which may be x per cent over today's productivity) – hence the need is for 10 salespersons.

It is at the unit and departmental level that we can analyse the individual and group changes in capability, and make a plan accordingly. There are six steps to the process at this level:

1. Do I know the business *objectives and milestones* for each major strategy? What is my reasonable *time horizon* for skills planning?
2. Do I have the suitable *diagnostic tools* to enable me to specify the knowledge, skills, attitudes and experience that the business both has and needs?
3. Can I therefore define *generic* shifts for particular groups, and *individual* shifts for each resource?
4. Am I able to evaluate the *learning capability* of individuals against these requirements?
5. Who can best provide me with the optimum *learning solutions* to meet specific learning objectives?
6. What then are my *resource planning decisions* between make (skill change), buy (recruit) or subcontract?

Step *1*: The strategic plan may be for three to five years, the operational plan for one to two years. Time horizons are important to consider – for example, if my plan is going to require many more general managers in five years' time, then I need all the time I can get to give planned experience towards their development. If my plan requires a progressive growth in a new market I will build up skills at the rate at which I get new contracts. This could give me a horizon as low as two to three months.

Step *2*: What is needed is a decision on the types of *roles* needed for the particular time horizon, and then a *role profile* which is a breakdown of the knowledge, skills, attitudes and experience required for those roles. Work in the UK from the Management Charter Initiative (for management in general) and National Vocational Qualification levels of competence (for specific types of job) may be helpful here, but it is more than likely that role profiles specific to your organisation will be needed. Matching individuals against such role profiles requires diagnostic tools which may come in various forms. They may be:

- specially constructed CVs
- self-assessed database matching
- independently assessed profiles.

Step 3: This is to define the 'generic' shifts that may be needed – that is, a shift in any learning dimension needed for groups – or indeed each individual – in the organisation. For example, it may be essential in the planning of the multinational merger that large groups of people go through a learning programme on multicultural understanding. Or it may be necessary to reskill whole teams to cope with a new technology.

Each individual needs a learning plan as well. In addition to areas of personal improvement learning or that which is future-career-oriented, the current role will require some development to meet the challenges that are coming.

Step 4: Not everybody will be capable of making all the capability changes needed, especially if they are 'step' changes. In a sensitive and counselling way we need to be sure of the capability of people before we launch them into an area where they are most likely to fail. Companies like IBM have moved thousands of people to the 'front line' – administrators, for example, who have never worked with customers. IBM's motivation was sound enough: move people to a greater added-value area and avoid the need to make them redundant. Yet many of those individuals, despite the training given, found it hard to make a success. In Schein's terms, 'their career anchors were elsewhere'.

Step 5: This is the choice of learning solution and provider. We discuss in Chapter 6 the range of learning methodologies available, and we should note that the provider may be within the context of the job rather than external to it. The setting of clear learning objectives, measurable when achieved, is a discipline that will pay back handsomely.

Step 6: With all the information above available one can now make resource planning decisions and set milestones for monitoring progress. In a Learning Organisation one should start with the hope that individuals and teams can be reskilled. If individuals cannot be re-profiled to the standard required in the time-scale available, one needs to make the decisions whether to hire or subcontract. This will depend on whether the skills needed are part of 'core' capability or not. One might also choose to subcontract temporarily if there is an urgent need but one's own people (assuming they are capable and willing) *need time to become competent..*

Following these steps, which need to be revisited every three or six months, should ensure the strategic objectives of the organisation will be matched by having the *right people with the right skills in the right place at the right time.*

 POWERPOINT

Does every part of your organisation have suitable diagnostic tools to match capabilities with business demands?

Does your organisation have a strategic planning process that recognises and defines the necessary human resource capabilities for success?

Is there a systematic process for skills planning that derives from the business plan down to team and individual learning plans?

Do the needs for investment in skills get built into the final business plan?

All other processes

The Learning Organisation has constantly to check its policies, processes and procedures to ensure that they are *encouraging* rather than *restraining* learning. This may bring conflict with the need to have sensible controls and reporting, and a balance has to be found. For each process the following 'Powerpoint' gives some indication of questions to ask.

POWERPOINT

Looking at all the key processes in your organisation which affect people:

Do they encourage rather than punish experimentation and risk-taking?

Do they put decision-taking as close to the point of impact of each decision as possible?

Do they trust people to use the organisation's resources sensibly?

Do they encourage sharing rather than reinforce tribal boundaries?

Pointers for action

The processes that people are subject to, or not subject to, in an organisation give powerful messages. They help or hinder managers and team leaders in implementing new aspects of culture change. For the Learning Organisation to flourish, many traditional approaches to people management have to be questioned. The effectiveness of collecting and providing feedback to individuals or teams, and the transfer of the implications into effective learning plans are a foundation of such an organisation.

Roles and the movement between them, including the basis of selection, need to be focused on how we use experience opportunities for learning. They need to be described in different ways to support this. Career management is no longer seen solely as rising through stages to higher levels in the organisation, but is about increasing personal value, and this is available to everybody *at all levels*. The focus on career progress in this way has to be matched by a reward system that reinforces the new and not the old.

The opinion survey is an effective tool available to help check from the employee's point of view what they think about aspects of the Learning Organisation as they experience it. Finally, disciplines of skills planning are essential to the resourcing of the business for the future.

The action that is needed overall is a comprehensive review of all the processes that are in place against the criteria that you believe describe the kind of Learning Organisation you would like to be. In addition it may be that some processes are needed which are not there at all. We use 'processes' rather than 'procedures' not because we imply anything bureaucratic here, but because we believe that some systematisation is of benefit.

Some of these changes require significant reorientation for human resources professional staff, as systems based on consistency and administrative efficiency are replaced by judgement, flexibility, and consultancy.

5

The Power of Information Technology

An organisational brain

How can an organisation learn when an organisation doesn't have a brain? Perhaps the question we should be addressing, more positively, is: can we create an organisational brain?

In small organisations, it is relatively straightforward to establish who knows what; people can rely on personal knowledge to get in touch with the right person and arrange a meeting to share knowledge and experience in the area of common interest. But as organisations grow and become more complex, it becomes impossible for any one individual to be clear on who knows what. Reinventing wheels – costly duplication of effort – is a common feature of large organisations, as is the danger of not learning from mistakes that have been made in the past.

Before recent developments in information technology, it was very difficult to maintain organisational memories and facilitate learning across the boundaries of large organisations. Academic institutions and the legal profession were probably the best examples we had of capturing past learning. Add global spread to overall size, and you have a very difficult nut to crack. Add the challenge of learning from what your competitors, customers, and suppliers are doing, and the challenge might seem an impossible one to meet.

Technology has been developing at an enormous rate and our understanding of how it can best serve organisations has also increased. A number of firms are now beginning to demonstrate that it is possible to capture knowledge and learning and then facilitate their movement across organisational and geographical boundaries, giving them a real competitive advantage. The organisations at the forefront of this in the mid-1990s are the consultancy firms – not surprisingly, as their

115

only product is knowledge and its application to clients' problems. Some of their experiences, and those of a number of different organisations, are related below.

Technology for human beings

As we shall discuss in Chapter 7, much activity in organisations is team-based. Flexible teams that come together to tackle particular projects sometimes have the additional complication of team members based in different parts of the organisation and possibly in different parts of the world. A new development in information technology is aimed at enabling human beings to work together – to meet without meeting (face-to-face), to work from the same knowledge base, to communicate quickly and easily. This technological step forward, on which many knowledge-sharing processes are based, is commonly referred to as 'groupware'. Groupware is a generic name for software programmes that enable different people, wherever they might be located, to access and work on the same documents and information, and to communicate easily with each other.

Electronic mail is the foundation of groupware, enabling people to share information and communicate with one another. The concept of groupware goes well beyond 'e-mail', however:

- Both documents and images can now be stored, with image scanners capturing photographs, forms and drawings onto disk for instant retrieval and viewing.
- Electronic bulletin boards enable queries and messages to be communicated across an entire network and instant responses given.
- Documents can be produced and then commented on electronically by a range of people – eg a corporate strategy plan.

- Electronic diaries and meeting schedulers facilitate team-working.
- Desktop conferencing enables facts and figures to be discussed from diverse locations, with shared documents on desktop screens while telephone discussions take place.

Groupware helps to create 'global villages' within organisations; it saves a great deal of time that might otherwise have been spent searching for documents in files, cupboards, and desk drawers; it reduces the number of face-to-face meetings required for team activities down to the essential ones; and it makes team meetings easier by helping to schedule them. Above all it enables people to capture learning and knowledge in such a way that they can be shared with others.

 **POWERPOINT**

Does your organisation encourage its teams to exploit groupware applications for more effective interworking?

Has your organisation exploited information technology to support the sharing of knowledge across boundaries?

Creating an organisational memory

Think of all the knowledge accumulated through the years in your organisation. How can an organisation hold on to years of learning – including the learning done by individuals who have left the organisation? In these mobile times, with jobs for life an anachronism, a great deal of value goes out the door when an individual leaves to join another company. How can an organisation capture learning – that is, create an organisational memory?

Information technology comes into its own here, with the ability to hold and search vast quantities of information. What information might be a source of competitive advantage for your organisation? Some topic areas that have already been developed into accessible databases in a number of organisations would be:

- the skills of people within your organisation: if you know what they are, you can put the right people with the right skills onto particular customer projects
- expertise registers: a database of organisational experts in particular topics, perhaps within your key functions
- market information: trends, competitors.

In addition to factual databases, there is great value in capturing learning that has already taken place. Examples of these types of databases would include:

- customer bids, proposals, reports: a record of your previous experiences will keep everyone in your organisation high up on a learning curve created by others before them
- subject matter expertise: in order to develop your organisation's core competences – the things that truly differentiate you from other organisations and give you a competitive edge – you may wish to develop databases that capture what people have learned in the application of these core competences
- lessons learned from major or even minor disasters in your company's history!

The decision to create an organisational memory is the easy step. A whole infrastructure must then be put in place, requiring a great deal of thought and investment. Individuals will need training in using the systems and an incentive to input to the databases. The case study of Andersen Consulting at the end of this chapter demonstrates that it is all quite feasible – where there is a will, there is a way!

POWERPOINT

Do you have a means of capturing knowledge into databases accessible to everyone in your organisation?

They must be here somewhere

Just finding the particular skills you need is a challenge in large organisations. The well-established concept of a skills database is becoming quite sophisticated, aided by developments in information technology to enable you to find the skills you need for particular tasks. The consultancies are well advanced in this area and the business of a number of software firms is thriving on this capability.

One example comes from an American software company who provide a database tool that captures the CVs of everyone in an organisation in a common format. The programme has the flexibility to include areas in which people would like to develop skills as well as listing skills they have already acquired. The database can then be searched on the basis of key words (eg skills required for a particular customer project) and within seconds produce a shortlist of internal candidates to fit the requirement. Individuals are responsible for keeping their details up to date. Needless to say, anyone exaggerating their capabilities will soon be found out when invited to apply their skills to a particular task, so the system is largely self-regulating.

This type of tool makes the formation of flexible teams a much easier task than it might have been in the past. Any Learning Organisation must have data on the skills available to it – this information is as vital as the financial information that is much more commonly tracked.

⚡ POWERPOINT

Does your organisation hold a skills database?

Does your skills database enable you to list learning/development needs as well as skills acquired?

Is it used regularly to bring temporary teams together to address customer requirements?

Does it enable you to assemble teams of people from different parts of the organisation?

Just-in-time information

With the fast pace of the business world today, learning requirements are sometimes immediate. If a customer requires a service or some information quickly, a top-service provider will respond immediately rather than spend three or four weeks trying to find the information. In a large organisation, particularly a global one, the ability to *leverage the knowledge across the entire organisation* is a powerful tool. An increasingly common information-technology-based tool is the use of electronic bulletin boards to ask for help or information. In 1991, some innovative technical people in the computer company ICL established an electronic network across 1,500 members of ICL's technical community worldwide. Dubbed 'Earwig', this system uses ICL's global electronic mail network as the basis for sharing knowledge across a professional community. Anyone with a query on a technical subject can input it to Earwig and instantly tap into a knowledge base of 1,500 experts. Despite the somewhat unappealing name, this electronic learning exchange is widely used and saves hours of individual research and experimentation.

McKinsey and Company, the strategy consultants, invested within one segment of the firm in a piece of technological infrastructure that is seen as a leading-edge initiative in the knowledge-sharing arena. Known as the 'Rapid Response Network', the system links ;

- an enquiry-tracking system
- a worldwide database of McKinsey work in that area
- a database of written documents relating to the subject
- a register of experts.

All of this is maintained and operated by a team of people who guarantee that any McKinsey consultant making an enquiry into the Network will have a response within a few hours. In this way the consultants can access the firm's total knowledge base to the benefit of their clients – and do so very quickly. One of the principal reasons for the success of this initiative is undoubtedly the people dedicated full-time to the process – often a critical success factor in these global, computer-based endeavours. Not surprisingly, McKinsey's have a top level partner whose title – director of knowledge management – indicates the importance they place on knowledge-sharing.

 **POWERPOINT**

Do you provide the infrastructure for and encourage the use of electronic bulletin boards to facilitate knowledge-sharing across your organisation?

Do you take information-sharing seriously enough to invest in a senior person or team accountable for making it happen?

Just-in-time learning

Having explored some of the advanced knowledge management processes that have been put into place, the more traditional form of learning – namely training and development – should not be forgotten. Great strides have been made in making training more flexible and better tailored to the needs of the individual – and information technology has had a role to play here as well. Computer-based training has been around for some time now. Its first major application was in technical product training but it has been extended into many areas of training, including management skills and language training.

Although computer-based training has brought training to the desktop of the person needing it, its early forms were not the most stimulating of learning technologies. Advances in multimedia technology have now made to-your-desktop training a much more interesting experience and therefore one likely to have a greater impact on the individual.

Multimedia training started with interactive videos, which enabled users to interact with a video programme and select particular courses of action. The videos would then demonstrate the result of making that particular choice. Interactive videos required an investment in special video players and tended to be provided in special resource or learning centres, to be booked by individuals. Phil Lingard, finance director at Futuremedia, a leading supplier of multimedia products, says that 'there is likely to be an explosion in the use of multimedia products as soon as the technical standard for multimedia personal computers is agreed'. This agreement is imminent and means that the prospect of PC-users having multimedia training products 'on demand' to their desktop is a very likely one. The principle is similar to the idea already being developed of 'video on demand' to home televisions.

A sample of this self-managed learning can be found at IBM's Education Centre in La Hulpe, Belgium. The bedrooms in the accommodaton blocks are each equipped with a personal computer that allows access to several computer-based training packages and interactive video products, as well as office applications, electronic mail, the hotel message system, and satellite television. We may soon find similar 'learning stations' both on our office desktops and in our homes.

The Dutch bank ABN–AMRO, an organisation of 45,000 employees, has made significant investments in educational technology. Their computer-based systems offer staff members a menu of choices from which they pick the modules relevant to their work. The software includes a self-assessment tool to enable the individual to decide where to focus. The multimedia-based modules are available at local learning centres to minimise time away from the job. Rather than describing this infrastructure as training, they call it their 'Electronic Performance Support System'.

If the potential of the technology is achieved, 'just-in-time learning' will be a crucial part of a Learning Organisation's infrastructure – and a big step forward from 'just-too-late' training!

⚡ POWERPOINT

Do you use multimedia and other technology-based training approaches for your organisation, where they are the cost-effective solution?

Do you have learning resource centres available to people in your organisation?

COGS and LOGS

The usefulness of technology-based training depends on individuals having identified the specific training and development that they need. Here too, technology can help. Software-based self-assessment tools can help individuals to identify both overall career options (through Career Option Guides, or COGS) and learning options to help them progress towards a specific career goal (through Learning Option Guides, or LOGS). Some software tools, such as the MIDAS package produced by Advanced Personnel Technology (APT), enable skill and knowledge requirements for particular roles within your organisation to be compared with the skill and knowledge profiles of individuals. By making this type of tool available to individuals within the organisation, employees can take charge of their career planning and build a much clearer picture of the gaps within their own portfolio of skills, knowledge and experience.

Having identified specific gaps, a Learning Options Guide can point the individual towards particular development options to meet the need identified – with the benefit of exposing the range of options beyond the classic training programme, many of them more cost-effective. Our chapter on individual learning gives an example of an entry from a paper-based Learning Options Guide – prepared to support ICL's 'Investing in People' programme, which was revised and made electronic in 1994. ABN–AMRO built a Learning Options assessment process into their Electronic Performance Support System – an obvious way to ensure an optimum return on their investment in technology-based learning.

 **POWERPOINT**

Do you make available software-based Learning Option Guides and/or Career Option Guides for individuals in your organisation, to enable them to plan their own learning and development?

Understanding your customers

Sharing knowledge and learning within a firm is an important process, but an even greater key to competitive advantage is learning directly from your customers. How can information technology help you to learn more about your customers' needs?

Benetton, the Italian fashion business, distributes its clothing through a network of Benetton franchises, owned and run by local managers but linked through a common computer network. Thanks to this capability, Benetton is able to track the precise buying patterns at particular branches and determine what styles and colours are selling particularly well. The manufacturing facility can respond almost instantly to the trends that are being spotted, and sends more of the styles and colours that are doing particularly well to the Benetton franchise that needs them. This is a good example of a very effective feedback mechanism from a market-place. A Learning Organisation must above all be learning about its market and its customers.

Price Waterhouse, the management consultancy firm, uses a software programme codenamed 'Sam' to track the work that its various consultants are doing with particular clients. This database, accessible to all, enables any Price Waterhouse consultant to check whether anyone else in the firm is doing, or has recently done, work with a particular client. Steve Redwood, a managing consultant in change management and a user of the system, says that:

> There are two main benefits. Consultants appear more professional to the client if they are aware of the other activities of the firm, and the database enables PW [Price Waterhouse] people to identify colleagues who can tell them what we have learned about a particular client before making an approach.

British Airways and other major airlines use its reservations database to keep track of customer preferences such as seating, meals, and preferred form of address, in order to give as personal a service as possible to its individual customers. Imagine how difficult this would be without computers keeping track of such information!

The use of information technology in learning more about your customers is an essential mechanism in a Learning Organisation.

 **POWERPOINT**

Do you exploit information technology in helping you learn about your customers' requirements?

Culture clash

In this information era, the free availability of data is more than just a technological shift. It requires a cultural shift within most organisations. Electronic networks like those described above cross organisational, geographical and hierarchical boundaries. Individuals who still feel that 'knowledge is power' and who try to limit rather than expand the sharing of knowledge will soon find themselves excluded from the spontaneous sharing of knowledge that is becoming a way of life. The President of the United States, Bill Clinton, made his electronic mail address publicly known, as a direct communication link with the people who elected him. President Roosevelt's 'fireside chats', using the medium of radio, were perhaps the previously best-known example of using technology to get close to the people. Now technology enables that communication to be two-way, even with people who were previously inaccessible.

Similarly, there is nothing to stop an individual at the lowest level of the hierarchy communicating directly with the chief executive through electronic mail. Middle and senior managers who are accustomed to being the gatekeepers of communication with their bosses will have to adjust to this new way of life; information on the business can in this way be shared throughout the organisation, reducing the need for the gatekeeper/communication roles which were common aspects of middle management roles. George McNeil, president and CEO of Bull Europe, wrote in *International Management* magazine in October 1993:

> Powerful personal computers . . . will be a conduit for information to flow around the company, giving employees the freedom to see, manage and pass it on as and when they wish to do so. Such a development in the use of computers will have important consequences for company culture: with information at their fingertips, employees will be in a position to take more and more decisions for themselves.

Price Waterhouse has implemented a number of information-technology-based processes to enable wider sharing of information across the firm. The phrase they have coined for their combination of technological and cultural shift is 'greater knowledge fully shared'. One of the pieces of information previously the privilege of the firm's partners but now available to all is the utilisation rates of individual consultants. Utilisation rates – the percentage of time being spent on chargeable activities with clients – are one of the key business measures of a consultancy business and also the key performance measure for individuals. Imagine the mindset shift required in accepting that this information is accessible to all! Despite the initial discomfort – partners having to be open about performance in their areas, individuals being open about their own productivity – the availability of this information is a powerful incentive to keep one of the key business measures healthy, as low performance can no longer be concealed.

 **POWERPOINT**

Do your employees have the information they need at any given time to make business decisions and track key performance measures?

Security issues

As with any technological advance, there can be drawbacks. In-company computer networks may be linked to external networks, so security of the data contained in knowledge management systems becomes an issue. An April 1994 article in the UK-based newspaper *The Guardian* stated the concern this way:

> . . . increasingly, ordinary people, of all ages and backgrounds, are discovering that a universe has been created, consisting of millions of interconnected computers, which may be the most anarchic and free place in human history. Unpoliced and unregulated, this communications network throws up questions about issues from civil liberties to commerce, sexuality to democracy. The debate now beginning about how far cyberspace should, or could, be patrolled makes our current concerns about video nasties, copyright law, the right to privacy and freedom of speech fade into insignificance.

Clearly security is an important issue with databases of knowledge, some of which may contain sensitive information relating to competitors or customers. There must be clear rules on who can access what, and indeed on what type of information can be placed in public knowledge databases. Customers will need to be certain that any privileged information is safe in your organisation's hands. Any internal network must have excellent security systems that prevent unauthorised access to the data; employees will need to sign confidentiality agreements that prevent them from taking key information with them if they leave your organisation.

POWERPOINT

Have you ensured that you have the right levels of security for your IT data?

Garbage In, Garbage Out

Another issue in knowledge management systems is the infamous 'GIGO' principle, which has always been a feature of computing: if you put Garbage In, you get Garbage Out. The quality of information going into the system must meet certain accepted standards or it will be useless. Poor quality information will lead to low use of the system which in turn will lead to poor quality of information. It may well be worthwhile identifying key people to manage the input of data to your knowledge management systems – as Andersen Consulting has done (see pages 130–1).

Another GIGO phenomenon is the problem of 'junk mail' on e-mail or electronic bulletin board systems. We recently heard of the example of someone who sent an electronic mail message regarding the dates of her forthcoming holiday to every user of the widely held Lotus Notes packages in her own organisation and across multiple-linked computer networks.

The man-hours that must have been wasted by thousands of individuals trying to work out who this person was and why she was telling them about her holiday must have been considerable!

 **POWERPOINT**

Have you established and communicated standards for the input to your information networks and knowledge databases?

Information overload

The junk mail problem leads to a more general issue: that of information overload. As more and more people are linked into information systems both at work and at home on an 'unpoliced' information superhighway, the volume of information can become so great that it gets impossible to pick out the important and relevant pieces of information. The time spent sorting through e-mails – the electronic equivalent of an in-tray – can easily take a couple of hours a day in large organisations where you can end up being included on far too many distribution lists.

Techniques are available to cope with this problem – ways of opting out of distribution lists or only getting information you request – but be wary of allowing knowledge management systems to add another thick layer of information to your organisation. Information overload works against the principles of a Learning Organisation: you either have no time to reflect on the information or it is irrelevant to the needs of your business.

 **POWERPOINT**

Do you have processes in place that direct information to the people who need it without creating information overload?

A picture of the possible

Some of the above may seem a bit far-fetched if you work in an organisation that is still somewhat technophobic. Tony de Bree, the ABN–AMRO Bank manager who put their Electronic Performance Support System in place, recognised the reality of technophobia among senior managers and provided each of ABN's top 200 managers with a personal portable computer on which to experiment with the new training technology, which smoothed the way for implementation. To try to emphasise how 'doable' it all is, we would like to share with you a case study of an organisation that is at the forefront of knowledge management and is demonstrating the art of the possible.

Andersen Consulting – a case study

One feature of the consultancy world is the reusability of knowledge: similar approaches, models, tools and techniques can be applied to different clients. Also, the experience gained in one client situation may make an invaluable contribution to the next client. Charlie Paulk, Andersen Consulting's chief information officer, responsible for information management across the firm's global operations, says, 'There is no longer such a thing as a "renaissance" consultant.' The breadth and depth of knowledge required to address the complex business issues that face Andersen Consulting's clients are greater than that of any individual. The firm has therefore made a strategic decision to leverage the knowledge of their global firm to help each individual consultant and his or her team provide high-benefit solutions to their clients.

Andersen Consulting conducted a research programme to determine how best to manage knowledge within the firm. The product of this research was an approach they dubbed the Knowledge Xchange™.

Wishing to practise what they preached, Andersen Consulting launched the Knowledge Xchange™ in 1992. The platform for this activity was a powerful worldwide information technology infrastructure and a number of related knowledge management processes. Having developed a technical architecture of networked personal computers and common software that would enable individuals across the world easily to communicate with one another, Andersen Consulting then encouraged interested service areas within the firm to pilot the process. Charlie Paulk described the overwhelming response they got: 'At the start of the process, we had about 600 people involved in pilots and about a half-dozen databases. In less than a year, over 6,000 people were involved and there were 150 databases in place.'

The databases to which Charlie referred covered a number of subject areas, depending on the needs of the particular group putting them in place. The most common focus areas were reference materials regarding best practices and methods; knowledge about current and previous projects; skills of individuals; and market intelligence. In addition, the information technology infrastructure made immediate knowledge-gathering possible: any consultant anywhere in the firm can send an enquiry over the network, asking Andersen Consulting's offices across the world for information or experience on any topic.

In addition to the technical infrastructure, a number of new knowledge management roles were created. These were as follows:

1. *Knowledge sponsor*: usually a partner, responsible for approving the set-up or deletion of databases within his or her area of activity
2. *Knowledge integrator*: responsible for designing a particular database and determining its links with other databases
3. *Knowledge developer*: responsible for ensuring that information is placed in particular databases.

Clearly an approach such as the Knowledge Xchange™ requires a great deal of careful planning and preparation before it can deliver real advantages to an organisation. Charles Paulk cites a variety of anecdotal evidence of the impact that it is already having, even this early in its implementation, and is convinced it will have long-term benefit for Andersen Consulting and its clients. The next area he is tackling is to ensure that the firm's use of the Knowledge Xchange™ is closely integrated with the client service process – like any major business process, it will not succeed in isolation.

Pointers for action

We believe that information technology is one of the greatest enablers of a Learning Organisation. Particularly in a large, complex organisation, it is unlikely that knowledge could be transferred and shared across global boundaries without a facilitating information technology infrastructure.

If you are daunted by the prospect of an enterprise-wide infrastructure such as Andersen's, consider this food for thought from a European-Union-funded project published in March 1994. In a report entitled *Technology, an Instrument for Learning Organisation Development*, the authors suggest that there are 13 learning-related processes to which technology can be applied in order to improve learning capability. These are:

- strategic planning
- resource allocation
- process management
- time and skill allocation
- customer feedback
- individual performance review
- team review
- sharing experience
- venturing
- innovation
- personal development
- individual learning
- internal collaboration.

Consider picking one or two key processes from the above list where you feel your organisation would benefit from some process improvement. Research some of the available technology – some of it will be software programmes available 'off-the-shelf' requiring minimal investment – and set up one or more pilots of technology-assisted learning. If your experiments are successful, you will convert the sceptics and the technophobes, and be able to build from there.

6

The Power of Personal Learning

Learning to learn

One definition of a Learning Organisation is an organisation
made up of individuals who are continuously learning. Much
has been written, very helpfully, about enhancing individual
learning; however, personal learning is a *necessary* but not
sufficient condition for a Learning Organisation.

Nonetheless, individuals within a Learning Organisation
must be learners. They must believe in the importance of
continuous learning and have the skills for it. If their learning
is in line with the requirements of the business, then the
organisation has a much better chance of having the right
people with the right skills in the right place at the right time.
The *individuals* will benefit by improving their employability.
And they need to take prime ownership for their learning and
be empowered to do so.

The incentive of employability

The natural curiosity and ability to learn that are so visible in
young children – as they learn to crawl, walk, talk, socialise,
play, write – seem to lessen with age. Perhaps the emphasis on
teaching rather than learning in many of our schools is one of
the factors that lead people to *wait to be taught* rather than to
seek to learn. By the time someone joins the world of work he
or she will have spent at least 12 years in an environment that
in many cases has expected them to be passive rather than
active in the management of their own learning. Organisations
compound this problem by being course-oriented rather than
learning-oriented. Also, there is an unfortunate perception
that once school and university days are over, the 'education'

phase of life has ended. Nothing could be further from the truth.

Restimulating that natural human desire to learn and then putting support in place to meet learning needs are major responsibilities in today's Learning Organisations. The disappearance of the jobs-for-life company and the reality of two to three career changes in most people's working lives mean that knowledge and skills must be kept up to date. *Employability* is the key; people may not expect to spend their whole career in one organisation but they do expect their work opportunities and challenges to increase their overall employability. There is a need for organisations to recognise this new reality – for example, in career development discussions, options outside the current line of work and the current organisation should be openly discussed.

 **POWERPOINT**

Is the concept of increasing people's employability openly discussed in your organisation?

Is one of your organisational objectives to offer challenges and opportunities to increase people's long-term employability?

How do people learn?

Much has been written about how human beings learn, and we do not intend to go into the detailed theories about this here. It is however important for individuals in a Learning Organisation to have a shared understanding of what learning is – and unfortunately this basic requirement is often overlooked.

Professor D. Kolb of the USA, one of the foremost figures in this field, gave this definition in *Experiential Learning*:

> Learning is the process whereby knowledge is created through the transformation of experience.

Figure 6.1
The learning cycle

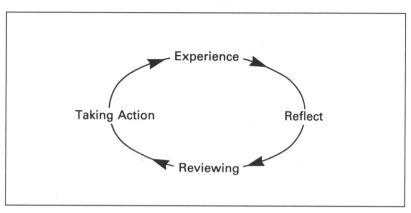

Alan Mumford in several writings has probably argued the case for a 'learner-centred' approach more than anyone. We like his very practical definition:

> A manager has learnt something either when he knows something he did not know earlier, and can show it; or he is able to do something that he was not able to do before; or both.

The key is the transformation of experience into knowledge and action. The learning cycle also needs to be understood. Honey and Mumford's presentation of it is shown in Figure 6.1. Learning has not taken place until the cycle is complete. Indeed, several cycles may be needed.

Also, different people learn in different ways or have preferred learning styles which relate to the elements of the learning cycle.

The simple recognition that *different people learn in different ways* is one that needs acceptance in a Learning Organisation. There are three main actions that need to be taken:

- Give people the opportunity to discover their most natural learning style.

- Offer learning opportunities that suit people with different learning styles.
- Recognise the need to complete the full learning cycle.
- Help people to translate the learning cycle into an upwards continuous spiral of learning.

Honey and Mumford suggest that there are four main learning styles, which are summarised below:

Characteristics of different learning styles

Activists:
- try anything once
- tend to revel in short-term crises and firefighting
- tend to thrive on the challenge of new experiences
- are relatively bored with implementation and longer-term consolidation
- constantly involve themselves with other people.

Reflectors:
- like to stand back and review experience from different perspectives
- collect data and analyse it before coming to conclusions
- like to consider all possible angles and implications before making a move
- tend to be cautious
- actually enjoy observing other people in action
- often take a back seat at meetings.

Theorists:
- are keen on basic assumptions, theories, models and systems thinking
- prize rationality and logic
- tend to be detached and analytical
- are unhappy with subjective or ambiguous experiences
- like to make things tidy and fit them into rational schemes.

Pragmatists:
- positively search out new ideas or techniques which might apply to their situation
- take the first opportunity to experiment with applications
- respond to problems and opportunities 'as a challenge'
- are keen to use ideas from management courses
- like to get on with things that have a clear purpose.

In Mumford's studies only 20 per cent of groups of managers came out with at least three strong preferences, ie were good all-round learners. In contrast 35 per cent had one strong preference. So standard prescriptions for learning will clearly not be as effective as custom-made structured experiences taking account of both the need and the style of the learner.

Research by Mumford into the influences that chief executives see as the most important in their own development highlighted:

- *early* responsibility
- *early* leadership experience
- a *breadth* of functional experience
- being *stretched* by their bosses.

They also listed several personal characteristics such as a need for achievement and an ability to negotiate off-the-job managerial training was bottom of the list.

It is helpful to ask yourself to recall a variety of learning events over the years and ask which were the most effective in enhancing your own professional profile, and which were the least effective.

The objective of learning is to *cause some change* – to enhance one's own effectiveness or the effectiveness of others, to change values and attitudes, to have experiences that are going to be drawn on in the future. Let us note therefore that a learning experience is not complete until it has had real and immediate application to the practical job situation and can be seen to be effective.

We observe many keen individuals burning midnight oil on part-time MBAs and then being very perplexed on graduation that their organisation does not seem immediately to recognise their achievement. Their manager can only observe what they do day to day, and there is rarely any immediate change in behaviour as a result of the studies. And so it is for many classroom experiences, especially in management development. Management trainers have become more creative and innovative in their methods over the years, including simulations and exercises – but only if there is a very real association with reality are they likely to be effective.

Clearly, individuals with natural tendencies towards a particular learning style will learn most effectively under the appropriate circumstances and approaches. For example, an Activist would get very frustrated listening to lectures. A Reflector would be uncomfortable being thrown in the deep end and expected to produce an instant response. A Theorist would be unhappy in a very unstructured learning environment. A Pragmatist would become impatient when there was no clear link between a training course and the current business issues. In a Learning Organisation, different learning styles are accepted and catered for.

 **POWERPOINT**

Does your organisation offer people the facility to assess their own learning styles?

Does your organisation cater for different learning styles in the development opportunities that it provides?

Moving from training to learning

We have already emphasised that most learning comes from experience rather than formal training. Yet one of the measures used by businesses who believe in investing in the skills of their people is the number of training days per person per year. Although this may be a significant step on the road to becoming a Learning Organisation, it ignores the fact that training is only one way of learning – and indeed that training events are not always the best way to learn.

To achieve the speed necessary to keep skills up to date in this fast-changing world, every possible learning method needs to be called upon. Many of them – such as coaching – are far more cost-effective than residential training events. The path from being training-focused to learning-focused looks something like this:

The TDLP scale:
from Training to Development to Learning to Performance

Training optional and *ad hoc*
Training mandatory and measured in days per person
Impact of Training reviewed and evaluated
Individual Development plans established for all
Learning methods expanded to include coaching, projects, etc
Learning measured and rewarded
Learning an integral part of Performance management

Until an organisation moves towards the 'learning' end of this scale, there is a danger that a great deal of time and money will be wasted on training events that ultimately have no measurable impact on the skills requirements for the business. Also, traditional training can perpetuate the culture of dependency that often develops through the schooling years – being often classroom-based, with the trainer deciding the agenda. The participant- or learner-centred events that progressive training and development organisations offer are a step in the right direction and, combined with an investment in follow-through and evaluation, can make training a valuable learning option. This is simply a note of caution: do not assume that because you invest a great deal in training, you have a Learning Organisation.

 **POWERPOINT**

Does your organisation focus on learning and its link to performance rather than simply training?

Creating a Learning Options Guide

Once a particular development need has been identified, the range of learning choices available to an individual can be very wide. However, because of the old-fashioned reliance on traditional training, many of them aren't even considered. Learning (or Development) Option Guides are a way of educating both managers and individuals on the range of learning opportunities available to them. ICL created such a Guide (referred to as a LOG) to support the key criteria that underpin effective performance (see table below).

ICL Learning Options Guide (extract)

Criterion: analytical ability
Definition: relating and comparing data from different sources, identifying issues, securing relevant information and identifying relationships
Coaching: ask the individual's advice when problem solving, eg 'What do you see as the issues here?'
Job Content/Projects: ask the individual to carry out an analysis of a business problem
Group activities: identify and initiate improvements in processes involving the team
Reading: *Management Decision Making*, John Adair, Aldershot, Gower, 1985
Other: encourage the individual to play chess or bridge!

There are similar entries in the LOG for 30 different skill/behavioural criteria. These Guides are provided to managers to help shift the emphasis from training to learning.

Clearly this line of thinking can be extended to any subject. You might like to supply:

- registers of expertise so people can request coaching from specific individuals on specific topics
- the set-up of action-learning teams around projects critical to your organisation that would develop the skills and knowledge of the people involved in them

- reading lists (very helpful)
- learning resource centres that offer the latest in flexible multimedia training technology.

The essential message here is *if you want people to move towards the management of their own learning, give them a map, a pathfinder to get them started.* Demonstrating that there are many ways to acquire skills and knowledge, only one of which is training, is a step along the way.

 POWERPOINT

Are people in your organisation aware of and using a range of development options?

Are managers in your organisation encouraging a wide range of approaches to people development?

Does your organisation support them with some form of Learning Options Guide?

Incidental learning

A Learning Options Guide can widen your perspective on learning but, as we have already stated, the greatest learning comes from experience. The 80–20 rule applics hcrc as wcll: 80 per cent of learning is on the job. The question here is how to maximise the learning that comes from experience. How can you ensure you don't make the same mistake twice? When something goes well, do you analyse why? When something goes badly, do you analyse why? Do you record in some way what you have learned so you don't forget it and so it can be shared with others? David Megginson of the Sheffield Business School has identified two blocks to effective individual learning: some people find it difficult to plan learning and others don't learn as much as they could from the experiences that they have. Yet both of these skills are crucial aspects of being an effective learner. What tools or techniques can assist?

The idea of keeping *learning logs* is no longer as far-fetched as it might once have sounded. A learning log is simply a record of what you have learned – perhaps at a meeting, or a training event, or in a particular week. It is perhaps simply jottings on a sheet of paper that make sense to you. A personal diary or journal can be a form of learning log. Tony Benn, the British Labour politician, is known to record meetings that he attends on tape and then play them back to reflect on the points he has drawn from them. He then writes his learning points every night into a personal journal which eventually turns into a book – so he could be said to be living his life three times over! Although very simple mechanisms, learning logs are a way of instilling a learning discipline. Andrew Gibbons, one of the proponents of learning logs, has one sheet per experience and records the following information:

- date
- description of experience
- what happened
- conclusions
- actions.

Without a recording mechanism, what is the 'half-life' of a lesson learned? How long does it stay with you?

For an individual to be an effective learner, techniques such as learning logs are helpful in that they encourage time for reflection. If you look at the classic learning cycle, reflection is a key part of the process. Yet the world is moving so quickly that few of us have time to pause and reflect.

There is an analogy here with the 'total quality' movement, which encourages people to seek the root cause to a problem rather than going for the quick fix. The quick fix in learning terms is what has been called single loop learning: you identify the problem and find the fix. Chris Argyris coined the phrase 'double loop learning' to describe the equivalent of looking for the root cause: something goes wrong, you determine how to fix it but then go further to question why you were doing it in the first place.

Double loop learning is crucial in a Learning Organisation. Individuals must question the status quo, go back to root causes, always ask the questions 'why?' and 'so what?'. Otherwise the organisation will stagnate, get complacent, or get very good at doing one thing when their market needs something else.

 **POWERPOINT**

Is taking time to reflect on lessons learned acceptable and encouraged within your organisational culture?

Are lessons learned shared with others?

Are people in your organisation encouraged to question the status quo?

Do changes take place as a result of this questioning?

Learning from life

When making recruitment or selection decisions, it is interesting that employers have tended only to consider the learning that has come from work experience. Similarly, individuals might invest a great deal in the development opportunities offered to them at work but often ignore the multitude of learning opportunities in other environments.

What skills can be developed by being a school governor at your local school? What knowledge can be gained by running a major fund-raising campaign for a large charity? How does the responsibility of raising children change someone? A year travelling around the world might be a much better test of initiative-taking and self-reliance than many workplace experiences, yet people are often apologetic about what is seen as a 'gap' in their CV. Opportunities to acquire knowledge and skills abound: it would be unwise to restrict your view exclusively to the learning opportunities offered through paid work.

Nick Potts, when personnel director at Virgin Atlantic Airways, described the skills of some of their directors in a speech at a conference in May 1994:

> None of us had classical CVs in the sense that most recruiters understand – but we all had done interesting and varied things. If you look at the three youngest directors, for instance, the commercial director has a degree in music and still gives professional recitals. He also was a quite talented motorbike racer. The marketing director has spent a lot of time boating . . . and the personnel director is an ex-professional opera singer! In fact we realised we had a lot of artists in all positions. This I suppose is not surprising as creativity, flair and imagination are very important in the Virgin culture. . . . You see we firmly believe that some are born to play the piano and some to carry it. We want the players.

Employers are being short-sighted too if they ignore the experience that people gain in the way they live their lives and contribute to their community. In a Learning Organisation the whole person is valued, not just the Monday-to-Friday commuter.

 **POWERPOINT**

Is the learning available from non-work activities taken into account in recruitment decisions?

Are people in your organisation encouraged to get involved in activities outside the workplace?

Are these activities recognised and discussed within the work organisation?

Action learning

Action learning approaches are an excellent method for ensuring that learning is directly in line with the needs of the business; we shall mention these again in Chapter 7 (on teams). Philips of the Netherlands has had such a system in operation for some time, known as the Octagon Program. Young high-potential managers are put into teams of eight to work on company issues outside their immediate area of expertise. They spend six to eight months on the task force and then make recommendations for action. The Octagon Program broadens their understanding of the company and its different components and also gives them an opportunity to work in cross-cultural groups. Importantly, they have a sense of being part of company decision-making.

Motorola brings groups of up to 30 senior managers together as part of their executive education programme to address major cross-company issues. After a one-week kick-off event, they break into smaller teams to tackle components of the issue. They like to think of this process as a 'learning lab', which fits in well with their R&D culture. Deborah King, director of Motorola's Executive Development Unit, says her ultimate objective is to 'make executive education invisible' by having it totally integrated with business issues.

Although action learning is usually a team-based activity, it has many learning benefits for the individual – strategic thinking, problem-solving, analysis, teamwork – and has the advantage of being directly linked to the needs of the business.

 **POWERPOINT**

Does your organisation use action learning to develop individuals and the business?

Self-managed learning

The complexity and constant change we now experience make the business of keeping skills up to date a difficult one. The personnel profession may use 'manpower planning' tools and 'development needs analysis' to try to understand the requirements and engineer the shifts required. Knowing that you will need 25 people skilled in the use of the automated equipment for your new factory is a relatively easy skills shift to make happen. However, in a world where no one quite knows what the future holds, when technological advances are made month by month, when organisations are changing shape radically and outsourcing whole chunks of their business, it becomes much more difficult to plan and implement the skills shifts that support your business.

Managers and HR departments are struggling to identify skills-shift needs and then to implement them with the right individuals, as the future is so ambiguous and unpredictable. Yet they would agree that *adaptability* is a key capability in this changing world and that every individual must re-profile their skills on an ongoing basis in order to remain an asset. The solution, it seems to us, is to turn the issue over to the people most directly affected: the individuals who make up the organisation. They have a direct motivation to keep their skills marketable: employability is becoming a key motivator. Armed with the knowledge of the organisation's overall direction, they are in direct control of their own learning and can invest time and effort in the areas that fit in with their personal interests and ambitions while responding to the organisation's business needs.

Consider these two different scenarios. An IT business is shifting from being a hardware maintenance organisation to a service organisation. The hardware engineers will need to learn to sell their expertise and skill to customers rather than to be called in to fix products, since the reliability of products has increased dramatically. Their traditional skills are engineering, not selling. The HR department agrees with the management team that a series of re-profiling courses are in order. All the engineers are put through the courses, with mixed results depending on individuals' aptitude for, or their interest in, the new skills.

Now consider this alternative approach in the same organisation. All of the hardware engineers are put through a diagnostic event which helps them to identify their skills, strengths and weaknesses and to analyse where they might like to take their career. A picture is then presented to them of the shift taking place in their business and the types of skills that will be required. They then individually decide how to take their own development forward. The individuals to whom these new roles appeal decide to invest heavily in their own training and development – particularly in sales techniques and how to become consultants. The people who feel they want to continue working with products decide to look for roles in other organisations where this is still an option. Some individuals might come to the conclusion that now is the time to set up their own business, perhaps with some initial support from the parent organisation. In each case the individuals are highly motivated to follow the paths they have chosen – precisely because *they* have chosen them. They make informed decisions based on the shared understanding of business direction.

Self-managed learning processes need to be part of the fabric of a Learning Organisation. If every individual in that organisation is taking full responsibility for his or her own development, the organisation has a much greater chance of keeping up with the times. A small group of personnel people and managers trying to engineer skills shifts – as though people were machines that could simply be retuned – is much less likely to achieve the desired results.

ICL has invested heavily in these processes since 1992 and although each business may design a slightly different variant, the overall approach has been as described in the table below.

An Approach to Self-Managed Learning (SML)

1. Senior managers meet to agree an overall business framework to share with the rest of the organisation. This framework becomes a key component of the diagnostic events that follow.

2. Groups of individuals (usually peers from across the organisation) go through a diagnostic event that helps them look at

themselves – past, present and future – and the business – past, present, and future. This is typically a two- or three-day residential event. They come to the realisation that there is no right answer, only likelihoods and trends, and only they as individuals can make the decision on the skills and experience portfolio they wish to build. They come out of the diagnostic event with a personal development plan.

3. Development groups of four to six people from the diagnostic event then meet regularly for a period of at least one year to support and encourage each person's own development. ICL has found peer pressure to be a very effective motivator to make something actually happen on the agreed development plans. The group members are sometimes selected on the basis of complementary skills and knowledge, enabling group members to coach one another and contribute to one another's learning. The groups are also good learning opportunities for becoming more effective at working in peer groups from across organisational and functional boundaries.

These development groups are assigned facilitators who encourage openness, help to build trust and advise on possible development options for individual needs. The groups meet regularly for at least a year and longer if they wish. The benefits of this approach are considerable:

- Individuals come to a shared understanding of overall business direction.
- The responsibility for skills development is put with the individuals themselves, with support from the organisation.
- Development plans are based on a high level of self-awareness and personal choice and therefore are more likely to be implemented enthusiastically.
- The process helps individuals *learn to learn*; in addition to short-term skills development, a long-term capability of continuous adaptation is built up.

Despite the benefits of the approach, there are some draw-backs:

- The process is extremely resource-hungry, in senior management time and facilitators.
- The diagnostic process does not achieve any skills shifts by

itself; the follow-on development activities must be invested in so that the skills shifts become a reality.

- When speed is of the essence and the required skills shift is relatively well identified, an SML programme is probably not the appropriate solution.
- The cost of three-day residential diagnostic events upfront is not necessarily a worthwhile investment for every individual; certain target groups might warrant this investment but other groups lower-cost methods such as self-assessment questionnaires, perhaps software-based.

Imagine an entire organisation composed of people who:

- understand their own strengths, weaknesses, aptitudes and interests
- have a shared understanding of business direction
- are motivated and supported in continually adapting their skills in line with business shifts.

The combination is a very powerful one. Putting in place the processes to achieve this is a critical responsibility in a Learning Organisation.

POWERPOINT

Does your organisation have processes to support self-managed learning?

Is there a shared understanding of business direction within which people can develop their skills?

Are your senior managers/leaders role models for self-managed learning?

Giving, not just taking

Self-development groups like those described above often involve the sharing of knowledge and skill between the members of the group. The link between individual and organisational learning starts at the point at which an individual shares learning with someone else. Therefore the emphasis on coaching needs to pervade a Learning Organisation, not just be the domain of managers.

People need to be rewarded for the knowledge they share; otherwise it is difficult to get rid of the old principle that 'knowledge is power'. For example, organisations that have implemented information technology systems enabling knowledge to be captured in accessible databases have in some cases rewarded people on their input to these databases.

The support and encouragement of formal or informal networks which exist to share knowledge are another way of giving individuals the opportunity to share their own experience with others. Involving members of the organisation in training events is another good way to tap the intellectual capital available.

 POWERPOINT

Does everyone in your organisation consider coaching to be an integral part of their role?

Does your organisation reward coaching behaviour?

Are a range of people – including line managers – from around the organisation contributing to training/learning events?

Are there many networks or special interest groups who meet to learn from each other?

Killing the sacred cows

You identify a problem, experiment and then find an approach that solves the problem. Not surprisingly, you might then feel that you had learned the right way to solve that particular problem. However, with the multiple changes around us, that solution probably has a relatively short shelf-life. In a Learning Organisation, 'getting set in your ways' is a danger to be guarded against.

One of the greatest challenges that face individuals in a Learning Organisation is *unlearning* ie the ability to accept that what seemed to be the right approach to an issue some years ago might no longer work (back to double loop learning again). One of the reasons that mature organisations seem to be less able to adapt quickly to market-place changes is the history and baggage that they carry with them. An organisation, like people, is after all a product of its history. How does a technology company transform itself into a service company? How does a centralised bureaucracy transform itself into a group of entrepreneurial businesses? There is as much 'undoing' to undertake as 'doing'.

At the individual level, how does someone who has progressed for 20 years on his technical ability suddenly unlearn that and learn to get ahead on his ability as a consultant? How does someone who strongly believed in the advantages of structure and processes suddenly unlearn that and see the benefit of less structure and more speed? If something worked 10 years ago or even five years ago, why wouldn't it work now? As with any change, the individual must believe there is a need to change and see the practical steps that he or she can take. Competitive pressures are now so strong that the need to change is usually uncomfortably clear to people – where they may need help is identifying the practical steps they need to take.

In a Learning Organisation, every individual has to learn, unlearn, relearn – nothing can be taken for granted. Being as unencumbered by history as the young child taking its first steps – or the new start-up venture down the road preparing to compete in your market – is one of the great challenges that face us all.

⚡ POWERPOINT

Are people in your organisation prepared to change or eliminate 'sacred cows' – things that are deeply embedded in the organisation as a result of history?

Pointers for action

Individual learning is one of the areas in which most organisations have made some kind of investment. This will tend to be an investment in *training*; we would encourage organisations to widen their view of individual learning opportunities well beyond this one methodology. Some initial steps to start the process might be:

- creating and sharing some kind of Learning Options Guide
- giving individuals the opportunity of assessing their learning styles to help them choose the most effective learning opportunities – perhaps as part of some of your existing training programmes
- putting a learning resource centre in place, with a variety of learning tools available
- ensuring everyone has a self-development plan as part of your appraisal/performance management process
- piloting a self-managed learning process for a group of enthusiasts.

training is still an important factor in developing new knowledge and skills. However, a Learning Organisation goes beyond specific skills shifts to the development of a core capability: the capability in every individual in the organisation to learn continuously and adapt effectively to the changes around them.

7

The Power of Teams, Networks and Communities

Team types

When was the last time you were in a team that really excited and energised you? If it was the football team at school, and no example from your work life springs to mind, then you are probably not alone in business organisations. Instead of the whole being greater than the sum of the parts, organisations somehow seem to subtract value when they put people together. We can no longer afford this to be the case.

The culture of most Western organisations focuses on the individual. Reward systems are usually geared towards individual achievements; 'management by objectives' tends to focus on the objectives of one person at a time, cascading through the hierarchy; organisational politics is usually a question of individual egos vying for supremacy.

The Learning Organisation makes the assumption that several brains applied to a problem are more likely to solve it than one. As Katzenbach and Smith put it in *The Wisdom of Teams*:

> the team is the basic unit of performance for most organisations. It melds together the skills, experiences, and insights of several people. It is the natural complement to individual initiative and achievement because it engenders higher levels of commitment to common ends.

In addition, teams are an obvious vehicle within which learning can be transferred between individuals; it is perhaps the most common point at which individual learning starts to become organisational learning. It is therefore crucial for Learning Organisations to encourage high-performance teams, as this will have two important effects:

153

- the application of a greater pool of knowledge and skill to particular business issues, thus improving the quality of the solution
- the improved transfer of knowledge and learning between individuals within a team.

Teams are vital components of a Learning Organisation – we will look at ways of making them work for the benefit of both the team members and the organisations to which they belong.

Informal *networks* of people with common interests, an increasingly common feature of today's organisations, are another mechanism for transferring learning. Think of the networks of which you are a part as we examine how networks can contribute to the effectiveness of a Learning Organisation.

As organisations flatten the hierarchies, something larger than a team but smaller than a network is appearing. For example, the heads of business units who might previously have been clustered into groups reporting to different directors might find themselves all reporting to the CEO in a flattened organisation. Or the functional groupings – finance, marketing, personnel – might lose their co-ordinating HQ structure but still retain their common professional interests. To distinguish these groupings from true teams (who are focused on a common objective) and from informal networks, we refer to them as *communities*. We will also explore the characteristics of these organisational clusters and consider how they might facilitate the sharing of knowledge and encourage organisational learning.

What is a team?

There are many different definitions of the word 'team'. For our purposes, we will define a team as *a group of individuals working collaboratively with a shared purpose*. Teams take many forms, as described in the table below ('Teams in the Learning Organisation').

Teams in the Learning Organisation

Team type	Purpose
Management team	Direction towards overall organisational goals
Work team	Specific accountability within the organisation
Project team	Accountability for a specific goal; likely to be a temporary grouping
Quality circle	Common goal of continuous improvement
Steering committee/Advisory board	Guidance towards a specific goal
Self-development group	Challenge and support of each other's learning objectives
Bid team	Putting together a contractual revenue-earning bid
Exploratory team	Investigating new possibilities such as an acquisition, JV or new market

Much has been written about teambuilding and the skills necessary to make a team effective. The point that particularly interests us here is: how can teams become effective vehicles for organisational learning?

Creating a teamwork climate

Creating a supportive organisational climate for teams makes good business sense. Teams have the tremendous advantage of assembling the right portfolio of skills and knowledge to apply to a specific issue, whereas individuals are limited by their own capabilities and background. This recognition that teams are a powerful tool for tackling today's complex issues is an essential step in any Learning Organisation.

The first task for an organisation wanting to maximise the impact of teams is to eliminate the blockers that inhibit successful teamwork. The formation of teams should be a fluid, dynamic process based on the customer requirements that arise: there should be virtually no restrictions on who can be invited into particular teams, as the mix of skills to achieve a result should be the main driver. This means breaking down some of the traditions where managers feel they 'own' individuals for their own purposes, rather than seeing them as an organisational resource to be applied to issues from different sources.

The results of teamwork should be publicly recognised; it should not be a question of the boss taking credit for the work of his or her subordinates. Mainstream organisational work is starting to be recognised much as it has always been in television and films: the credits should roll and include everyone who had an impact on the final product. Quality or excellence awards are for teams as well as individuals.

We need to get cleverer at setting team objectives; there is no reason why management by objectives should apply only to individuals. For example, why not set a shared objective for a group of individuals whose task is to achieve the objective? They can determine amongst themselves how to split the work and then each be measured on the same end result. This is the very principle on which 'self-managed' teams are based.

The ability to work effectively in teams is a skill that, like any other, can be developed. It should certainly be an aspect of discussions on personal development. Individuals' ability to operate in a team environment should be a criterion for both selection and promotion.

 **POWERPOINT**

Does your organisation recognise the value of teamwork explicitly: for example, are quality improvement awards or other visible recognition mechanisms awarded to teams as well as individuals?

Does your objective-setting process include the possibility of setting team objectives, not just individual objectives?

Do your criteria for promotion include the teamworking skills of individuals?

There are three main facets of teamworking which increase the *learning capability* of an organisation:

- the transfer of knowledge and skill between individual members of a team with different backgrounds
- the collective learning that a team goes through in working towards their common goal, such as the better understanding of the market-place that a task force achieves when researching a particular business opportunity
- the continuous learning that the team members experience in making teams more effective – in other words, process learning rather than content learning.

Learning from one another

Once a number of individuals come together as a team to work towards a certain goal, they must ensure that the potential organisational benefit of their combined skills is fully realised. The members of a team must apply their portfolio of skills to the task at hand and achieve a positive result. That will achieve in turn the business objective. However, simply applying their individual skills to the task at hand will not significantly increase the overall learning of that team. Team members must consciously coach one another and share expertise with other members of the team to create truly organisational learning. Coaching is now a recognised role of team leaders but it is equally important within the peer group.

A good example of this approach is the process which self-development groups go through. Self-development groups are small teams of people who come together to 'challenge and support' one another in their quest to develop their individual portfolios of knowledge and skills in line with their own ambitions and business requirements. Because they are formed expressly to deal with learning, the team composition is often based on people with complementary skills who can learn from one another. Facilitators of self-development groups will often encourage the participants to take advantage of the knowledge and skills within the group through coaching activities.

Coaching is equally valuable in a task-focused team working together to achieve a result. For example, a finance person working through the financial aspect of the task can easily share his or her thinking with an individual for whom finance is not a strength. This enhances the capability of that individual to deal with the next task where some understanding of finance may be required. The willingness to coach others must become a normal aspect of organisational life and a prerequisite for success in that organisation. It must therefore be evaluated, which might require mechanisms such as upward appraisals to be put in place.

 **POWERPOINT**

Are the opportunities for learning among the considerations taken into account when teams are composed?

Learning together

A team working towards an objective will inevitably learn as it goes along: market requirements will become clearer as research is undertaken; customer perceptions will be better understood as surveys are analysed; ways of influencing key decision makers will be found as the team experiments. In order for this process to make a real contribution to organisational learning, it is worth making it explicit.

In order to reinforce the learning for each individual, a

mechanism is required to highlight the learning points and embed the learning more strongly and consciously. Thus, a methodology often used in training should become a standard approach when working in a team: *taking time to review learning points as a group*. This type of review – which might take place when a particular task is achieved or after important milestones are reached – has the benefit of bringing out all of the learning that has come from a particular activity, which may differ from one individual to another. This process does not need to be overly formal or particularly time-consuming. It is simply a question of someone in the team (possibly but not necessarily the leader) asking: 'So what have we learned from all this, that we didn't know when we started?' Bringing out the range of learning points means that individuals each learn more than they would have done on their own.

The challenge, then, is to transfer this team learning to other teams, for truly exponential organisational learning. This is likely to require more formalised processes to transfer knowledge across boundaries (see Chapter 5).

Action learning

Action learning is a team-based approach which takes place in the context of tackling real business issues. There is a great deal of merit in assembling teams with that learning and development focus in mind. We have already suggested that this is an excellent approach for developing the skills of individuals seen to have senior management potential, developing both their strategic thinking skills and their ability to work collaboratively. However, we are suggesting that action learning is no longer the domain of management development specialists; action learning is now the only way to run a business. Every task and each team effort should be viewed as the learning opportunity that it is, by everyone involved with it. Processes for creative problem-solving in teams are a vital aspect of any Learning Organisation.

POWERPOINT

Do teams in your organisation take time to review learning points from the experiences they have as a group?

Are these learning points captured in some way and shared with others?

The art of dialogue

With the importance of teams in Learning Organisations, the effectiveness of team processes is an important contributor to overall competitive advantage. Like team learning, continuous improvement of team processes is something that shouldn't be left to chance.

The classic example of a team continuously reviewing and improving its own performance is that of a sports team. Athletes in a competitive team review each performance and ask themselves what could be improved for the next competitive event. This discipline needs to become a regular feature of business life for teams.

How often does a management team take time to review the effectiveness of its own processes? How often does a team ask itself: 'How could we have run that meeting better?' Yet simply asking these questions could have a considerable impact on the ability of the team to achieve results.

One of the common features of ineffective teams is the tendency for individuals to see decision-making processes as a sort of 'zero sum' game. When individual egos dominate, the name of the game is to win an argument, not find the best solution to the problem being addressed. Peter Senge differentiates between the two different skills of 'advocacy' and 'enquiry': the former is the ability to sell one's own ideas with the intention of 'winning the argument' and having them adopted; the latter is the skill of probing to the depth of an issue, building up on the ideas of others and exploring points of view until the best possible solution is found. A team-based approach to problem-solving is far more effective if enquiry skills are used, although advocacy has its place – as long as the difference between the two approaches is recognised. Only by exploring the way the members of the team interact can this sort of distinction become clear – and useful – to all.

An effective way of bringing out these team process issues is to weave them into workshops that are focused on business issues. In this way team members who may have little experience of exploring team dynamics and personal style issues may be more comfortable. The team members can be given the opportunity to evaluate their personal decision-making styles through a personal profiling tool such as the Myers-Briggs Type Indicator or Belbin team roles. This then gives them a common vocabulary to use on personal style issues. The effectiveness of team processes can then be discussed after sessions focused on the business task – enabling the participants to give real examples to support their points.

POWERPOINT

Is facilitation support available to teams in reviewing the effectiveness of their processes?

Boundary-spanning teams

As people in organisations become more skilled at working in teams, the challenges that face them will continue to grow. To tackle complex business issues, teams will often need to be created that go beyond the boundaries of the particular parts of the organisation, beyond hierarchy and indeed beyond the core organisation altogether. Customers, suppliers, competitors, strategic partners – there will often be times when teams will be composed of people from very different organisations. The skills required to handle these types of teams are similar to those that have always been needed when working in multinational teams: cultural sensitivity, an appreciation of the importance of language, the understanding of differences in style.

At INSEAD, the European business school, students attending the MBA programme are assigned to work groups at the start of each term. These work groups of six to eight participants are carefully composed of people with the widest possible range of backgrounds: nationality, work experience, language. These work groups must then complete a number of assignments in the course of the term; often these are analyses relating to business case studies. The experience of producing results in these multinational teams is probably one of the most valuable aspects of the INSEAD programme – and the challenge is not to be underestimated, even for a group of students believing themselves to be internationally-minded.

Working in multinational teams or teams composed of people from different organisations (eg customers and suppliers) is a tremendous opportunity for learning. Our definition of the Learning Organisation includes the need to 'harness the full brainpower' available to your organisation, some of which may be outside your immediate organisation. By developing the sensitivity and openness that anyone working in multinational settings must have, people in your organisation will be far more receptive to learning from others, rather than afflicted with the all too common 'if it's Not Invented Here we're not interested' attitude.

⚡ POWERPOINT

Does your organisation invest in developing cross-cultural sensitivity and related skills to support 'boundary-less' teams?

Do you involve external people – customers, suppliers, perhaps competitors – in your internal activities?

Do people involved in direct teamwork with people from outside bring the things they learn from them into the organisation?

Networks

As 'continuous employability' becomes the aim of individuals, identification with our professional community (eg management, accountancy, human resources, software development, consultancy . . .) becomes of equal importance to the link with our particular organisation. Attending a major European conference on leading-edge accountancy practices or innovative human resource development policies may be a bigger motivator for people in those fields than attending their firm's annual get-together.

Even within organisations, groups of people with a common interest are tending to bond together more strongly, often creating semi-formalised networks which may be completely outside the sphere of the official organisation charts. Encouraging such spontaneous networks is important within a Learning Organisation. These networks usually cross organisational boundaries and serve as a vital information highway for the people within them. Nancy Foy says in *Empowering People at Work* that:

> informal networks create windows in organisational walls
> without damaging the sense of membership of the people
> inside those walls . . .

Crucial benchmarking information, examples of best practice within the business, personal contacts for help and advice, a critical mass of people to effect change: networks offer all of these things. The conferences and workshops that were once dismissively referred to as 'jollies' or 'talk shops' may on the contrary be vital organisational learning, if used for that purpose.

Because professionals in a particular sphere tend to be part of external networks in their field, a network of professionals or people with common interests is in fact a mechanism for bringing a flow of external ideas and experiences into the organisation. It is likely to be far more cost-effective to support and encourage a network of secretaries and administrators,

say, who might compare notes on good administrative practices or the best way to negotiate rates with hotels and
conference facilities, than to refuse to give your secretary time
off to attend a meeting of the network, yet expect her to be
continuously improving the contribution she makes to your
department.

Networks are often ignored because they don't appear on
the traditional organisation charts that we imagine to be an
accurate picture of our business structure. Making real use of
these networks for the benefit of the business will be a key
feature of the Learning Organisations of the future – by
facilitating their meetings and capturing the learning that goes
on within them.

Some examples of the sort of networks that thrive within and
across most of our organisations are described in the following
table.

Living Networks
These include: • *professional interest groups*: customer service managers, personnel professionals, quality experts (these can be internal and/or external)   • *personal profile networks*: women managers, high-potentials/ fast-trackers, recent graduate entrants, working parents   • *old boy networks*: people who once worked together, people who went to the same school   • *expertise-sharing networks*: technical people in similar areas   • *social networks*: sports clubs, fund-raising networks   • *alumni*: people who attended a course/school together.

These networks relate back to the notion of 'tribes' that we
explored in Chapter 3. They are important constituents in a
Learning Organisation.

POWERPOINT

Does your organisation support and encourage informal networks?

Is there a mechanism for capturing and sharing the information
and knowledge built up by such networks?

Work communities

Even in flexible organisations where teams are assembled on a project basis, people still need to have a home base. These groups of colleagues do not necessarily share a common purpose in the way that a team does; for example, a group of consultants working in the same business domain may each be working for different clients on very different projects. Their 'teams' are the groups of consultants focused on one particular client at any one time. They do however share common interests and learning needs with their colleagues working in the same area.

Another example: when a layer of headquarters staff is removed, a collection of business unit heads may find themselves reporting directly to the chief executive. Each managing director may be responsible for his or her own business and those businesses may have quite different objectives; each individual would consider their 'team' to be the management team of their business. However, the 'colleagueship' with their fellow managing directors is also important. The individuals in that grouping can share experience relevant to their unique role in their businesses; they can share knowledge and skill in the form of people movement; they can identify opportunities for synergy and make the whole greater than the sum of the parts. A further example might be a group of legal specialists from different business units who share experiences, tackle common problems and invest in cross-community training programmes.

The characteristics of work communities are similar to those of social communities:

- The individuals will be very different personalities.
- They may choose very different paths in life.
- People are not always close or caring.
- Some members are more independent than others.

Yet just as social community members can give support to one another, work towards some common goals and help one another in times of need, people in work communities can also benefit from the support of their peers and colleagues. Effective collaboration within peer groupings can be another source of competitive advantage, but has been given far less attention than traditional teamwork.

The amount of energy spent on internal rather than external competition is costing many large organisations a great deal. The organisational support and encouragement of work communities form one way to make internal boundaries more transparent and build stronger peer linkages.

 **POWERPOINT**

Are work communities recognised as having added value for the individuals within them?

Is contact between members of a work community facilitated or encouraged?

Are their development needs as a work community considered?

Pointers for action

The complex challenges that face organisations are such that an individual acting in isolation is very unlikely to have a significant impact. Learning Organisations need to allow many forms of teamwork to flourish. Work teams, informal networks, work communities – each has a different contribution to make to the flow of knowledge across the organisation. Temporary teams are becoming an increasingly common feature of organisations, assembled for specific tasks by bringing the right people with the right skills into them, crossing organisational boundaries if necessary. The ability to find individuals with specific skill profiles quickly and efficiently for such teams is one of the challenges of a Learning Organisation (and is dealt with in more detail in Chapter 5).

Shifting to a more team-oriented organisation can be achieved in manageable steps, such as:

- recognising the existence and value of different types of teams, and supporting them by funding their meetings and giving individuals time to attend team/network/community events
- creating the organisational flexibility to assemble teams quickly with the right combination of skills – perhaps by piloting the approach in a designated part of your organisation, using a skills database as the major instrument
- in your recruitment, performance and reward systems, ensuring that the ability to work effectively in teams is a criterion you evaluate.

Anyone unable or unwilling to work collaboratively will be a blocker to the creation of a learning culture. Teamwork is the foundation for sharing learning – and a Learning Organisation will actively encourage and develop it.

8

The Power of Organisational Learning

How can organisations really learn?

There are two questions that face us here:

- What should we do at an organisational level to facilitate common learning and an environment that matches the needs of a Learning Organisation?
- How do we ensure that all the learning that is taking place with teams and individuals is harnessed for the good of the whole?

Swieringa and Wierdsma define the Learning Organisation as:

> one in which people learn through working together and work together through learning – and thereby are able to sustain their collective development.

'You can't shake hands with organisations', say these authors, but you can understand their components of strategy, structure, systems and culture.

Swieringa and Wierdsma observe that large, mature organisations (termed 'bureaucracies') are founded on rationality and logic, and solve problems by fine-tuning procedures or passing them up to the next level. Emotion is regarded as unhealthy, and the effect is to undermine many people's *courage to learn*. They note further that such organisations often have a large gap between what is said and what is done: a large amount of *talking together* is done and less *acting together*. Making mistakes upsets the system, and although they may not be overtly punished, the appraisal and reward systems do not encourage admitting to them at all. It is not easy to transform such entities into Learning Organisations as we have described them. Whereas reorganisation is frequent, more fundamental *behavioural change* to the systems and culture is rare.

As individuals in organisations continually learn, the sum of that learning harnessed collectively should be an even more powerful force. It is not always so. Situations arise where people collectively do what none of them actually wants to do individually at all. Or a line is followed because of the power of a particular personality, and is not bought into by others – who nevertheless feel they must take collective responsibility. One reason for this may be that the members have learnt different things in different ways at different times (which is natural and inevitable) *but learnt very little as a group together.*

We have discussed a number of these elements in earlier chapters, and now we want to look at aspects of the way organisations work that will help us with the two questions at the beginning of this chapter. We will look at the following areas:

- the influence of organisational structures
- the sharing of learning
- benchmarking competition and the 'best' comparative organisations
- learning from mergers, acquisitions and alliances
- adapting to change in the environment
- the power of learning and unlearning together.

The influence of organisational structures

Peter Drucker wrote in 1988:

> The typical large business 20 years hence will have fewer than half the levels of management of its counterpart today, and no more than a third of its managers . . . It is far more likely to resemble organisations that neither the practising manager nor the management scholar pays

much attention to today: the hospital, the university, the symphony orchestra. For like them, the typical business will be knowledge-based, an organisation composed largely of specialists who direct and discipline their own performance through organised feedback from colleagues, customers, and headquarters. For this reason, it will be what I call an 'information-based' organisation.

Drucker's vision has been reinforced with the immense progress in information technology. Yet many managers have not yet grasped the implications of this and still operate under a 'command-and-control' view of the world. Some are obsessed with structure, and their first perceived task on appointment is to 'set up my organisation'. Reorganisation is a frequently favoured response to a need for change and whilst powerful, it is never a solution to underlying business problems.

There is no perfect structure, and it should always be a balance with the capabilities available. Of course the utilisation of those capabilities in the most powerful way is an undoubted key to success. Well-defined roles with clear accountabilities are the essence of organisational effectiveness. However, certain approaches are much more supportive to the Learning Organisation than others.

Boundaries have great power in many organisations, and are strongest where the 'corporate glue' is weakest. Boundaries define the tribes and their loyalties, and work naturally against the Learning Organisation. The more self-sufficient and independent a unit is, the less it will feel any need to share and access the knowledge and experience of others. The needs of the business will determine more than any other factor where those boundaries should be set, but a Learning Organisation asks also where it is important that cross-learning occurs. Units who for years have vied with each other can miraculously begin to co-operate when they find themselves sharing common goals as partners in a new division, for example.

We want boundaries to be as transparent and fluid as possible for learning to be encouraged. Dependency on each other for achievement helps this considerably. Thus some organisations are deliberately changing from being vertical, hierarchically structured, functionally-oriented to becoming flatter, more horizontal, cross-functional. The basis is that an organisation should be customer- or project-driven, concentrating on processes that support the customer rather than those that support control by the top management. This is described by Ostroff and Smith, who use Motorola's Government Electronic Group as a practical illustration. Teams are formed around workflows *across* the organisation rather than around an individual task. Everyone is linked to the end result. Forums to discuss issues work across the whole process, whereas previously they would have operated vertically, with protective boundaries between functions.

Another way of weakening boundaries is to have *matrix* structures, where accountability for end results is shared between functions. A common example is a matrix of strategic/global line of business with geography. Asea Brown Boveri (ABB) is the classic example of a matrix organisation. A business manager may have up to three bosses, reporting on different aspects of his or her operation. Again, this encourages sharing of knowledge and experience across the organisation. Such structures work best where there is complete clarity and understanding of roles and accountabilities, and where the objectives of participants are not in conflict.

We would expect *boundaries* to be flexible, easily crossed and easily moved in the Learning Organisation, and to be places where intensive contact and *dialogue* take place. It is a mark of success in the organisation's own learning that boundaries will change as needed. These dialogues may be regular between key players, or informal and less frequent. Electronic applications help enormously to facilitate them. Someone in the organisation should take specific responsibility to ensure that they happen.

Layers of management have been another enemy of the Learning Organisation, as people in different layers have played with 'the power of information'. *De-layering* is a popular tool of organisational transformation today. Driven

primarily by economic pressures, it is strongly linked with
social and cultural movements designed to empower people,
release their energies, and place decisions closer to the point of
impact. Thus organisations move from being *pyramidal* to *flat*.
In a study by UK consultants Strategic People of 123 personnel
directors in March 1994, 80 per cent reported that they had
reduced layers, or were in the process of doing so. Of these
exercises 42 per cent resulted in greater numbers of people
reporting to one manager.

In his book *Intelligent Enterprise* Quinn shows that very flat
organisations can flourish where:

- localised interactive contact is important
- each operations unit can operate independently from others
  at its level
- the critical relationships between decentralised units and the
  centre are largely about information
- the majority of relationships with the information centre are
  routine and rules-based.

Examples are insurance selling, financial brokers, franchises,
and software workers.

Information technology tools can allow a 'span of communication' of several hundred people in suitable organisations.
Access is needed to co-ordination and to expertise. Thus in
Merrill Lynch in the USA, 17,000 branch office brokers
effectively all report to headquarters, with some local oversight
of activities. Through using electronic communications and
database access, the company has the capacity both to harness
the knowledge spread across the whole enterprise, and to
provide local personnel with access to this expertise base.

De-layering has the potential either to encourage or discourage learning, depending on how it is managed. Reduced layers
means reduced filtering and greater availability of information,
and probably greater sharing. It *supports* greater autonomy
and space – and these are powerful ingredients of experiential
learning. Reducing bureaucratic procedures frees people for

more interesting and worthwhile tasks. However, a manager certainly has less time to spend with individual employees. The theory that empowered people do not need direction, leaving the manager to concentrate on being a coach, is little more than that – a theory! Work does not redistribute itself that easily in reality. So this forces people to take more responsibility for themselves and their own learning. With suitable guidance, this is positive. However, if no parallel change occurs with the processes of appraisal and development, a major gap may occur.

Devolution is about reducing corporate staffs, minimising headquarters, and devolving authority to smaller and smaller self-contained business units. For large organisations it is a challenge to get the right mix of devolved units and yet maintain, first, seamless customer interfaces and, second, 'federal synergy' which exploits the benefits of the name and brand image of the organisation.

Devolution of authority gives more space for learning. There are dangers, however. Boundaries become stronger; incentives to share information for the good of the organisation as a whole may be minimal. Expertise and knowledge resident in the centre may be lost, and devolved units struggle over time to recreate their own knowledge and experience. Valuable learning positions which enable individuals with potential to spend time seeing the whole and how it works together, or to be ambassadors for the organisation externally, should not be lost.

Devolution reaches its extreme in 'starburst' organisations, where units are split off like shooting stars wherever it looks like a market-defensive business could be created. Freeing such businesses from all bureaucratic constraints is bound to be positive *provided that* the business itself is sound; if not it could be suicide. It suits fast-moving, innovative, knowledge-based organisations. If the 'starlets' begin to build their own overheads, and spin out too far culturally, some devolution may have to be reversed to reconsolidate organisational efficiency and synergy. Marcus Alexander of Ashridge Management College has specialised in studies of devolved organisations, and believes there comes a time when 'satellites' see their own need for more support. Cable and Wireless in the UK is one of the corporations that has looked for a new federalism and identity across its diverse subsidiaries. One way it has chosen is to have high-level, prestigious conferences of its top people from around the world, exposing them to external inputs from academics and industrialists, and working out together the lessons for the Group.

Team-based structures may result from any combination of the above. 'Spiders' webs', 'networked', 'clustered' and 'self-managed' teams are described as models of the future. Here, teams have contact persons with organisational expertise but otherwise manage their own objectives and interaction. Quinn sees what he calls 'Skunkworks Spiders' Webs' as particularly appropriate for design groups – a very informal organic structure ideal for innovation. (The term originates from the group that IBM set aside to develop their belated personal computer.) These types of organisation embrace relatively independent 'nodes' operating to performance contracts, and all are interconnected for communication and knowledge-sharing purposes. They suit many consultancy organisations. As we discussed in Chapter 7, opportunities for learning in such structures are significant. More *coaching leaders* are needed, and boundaries tend to be weaker than in old, functional structures.

A number of practical applications of such transformations exist and have been written about. Mills and Friesen describe the model created by BP Engineering, a centre containing 1,400 engineers and support personnel. It abandoned a traditional functional structure in 1990 and, after several steps along the way, now draws its chart as a series of clusters. These clusters are mission-centred rather than hierarchically controlled. Senior management control is through sophisticated data-reporting rather than supervision. The supporting functions such as finance, personnel and quality are *services* rather than pursuers of their own objectives.

Lars Kolind, president of the Danish hearing-aid company Oticon Holdings, describes his organisation as 'spaghetti-like'. Lacking all formal structure, it consists of individuals and teams who totally understand the strategy and the values, and with these alone determine their role and objectives autonomously. They have been extremely successful in their marketplace in terms of innovation, market share and profitability. The lack of structure and rules gives them very low costs. Visionary leadership clearly plays a large part in such an organisation (about 1,200 people) working so well.

It is unlikely that team-based organisations will completely replace staff and line divisions and hierarchy. Having some of these boundaries will be the most efficient approach in many organisations. A lot of literature assumes that the models can be applied in a pure form; but in most large organisations we will see pockets, hybrids and experimentation. It does not make sense to force an organisational style onto a leader who is not ready to cope with it. The Learning Organisation is characterised by the *flexibility* of its approach to boundaries, and recognises that every boundary – be it between layers, functions, businesses, staff and line, geographies, or whatever – needs to have mechanisms that exchange information and learning across it.

Quinn describes the *role of the Centre* in devolved and team-based organisations as 'raising resources, seeding core competencies, managing the culture, and setting priorities'. It is much less about control and detailed reporting, although it certainly needs regular information about each business. This can be systematised and electronic: fast-moving retail organisations know every morning what was sold in every store through totally electronic data collection, analysis, and presentation. The Centre's role is about setting values and strategy, and particularly about managing the sharing of knowledge and experience for the good of all its parts.

POWERPOINT

Is your organisational structure focused on maximising client responsiveness, innovation and learning?

Does it encourage teamwork and discourage functional and tribal boundaries wherever possible?

Are supporting functions primarily providing services, sharing information and adding value?

Where there are boundaries in the structure, are they transparent, and are there mechanisms for dialogue (both formal and informal) to take place across them?

Sharing learning

'In the Nokia Group, knowledge is power only when it is shared', wrote CEO Jorma Ollila in his 1993 Annual Report quoted earlier. As we discussed in Chapter 3, boundaries and power politics get in the way of sharing learning, and there is a fundamental need for a *willingness* to share knowledge and experience. This is absolutely vital if a Learning Organisation is to be maximised, and the rewards for stakeholders are to be realised. It is our conviction that information technology provides powerful tools to aid this, and combined with an *internalised value* of its importance to everybody in the organisation will go a long way towards success. Ensuring this happens is an essential leadership role.

Nature shows us an example with the way blue tits manage to select those milk bottles on UK doorsteps that are 'full fat' milk, in order to peck through the tops to get at the milk. We don't know how they choose the right ones, but we do know they can do this as a species when others can't. The reason is thought to be that blue tits move from flock to flock and pass on their techniques, whereas other more territorial species do not have opportunities to share their learning.

Here we want to look more specifically at the mechanisms

Figure 8.1
Organisational learning model

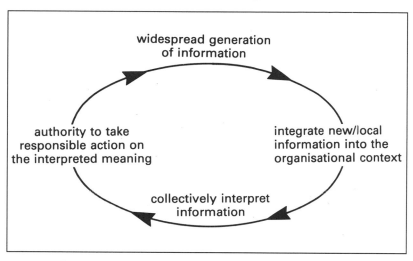

Source: Nancy Dixon, *The Organisational Learning Cycle.*

for making the learning that an individual has received more widely available. Nancy Dixon describes a virtuous cycle or organisational learning (see Figure 8.1). In many organisations the steps of generating, integrating, interpreting and acting on information are resident in different functions.

The *generation of information* occurs externally or internally in numerous places. Burgoyne, Pedler and Boydell talk about 'boundary workers' as 'environmental scanners' – the many employees who have direct contact with customers, suppliers, the community and others with relevant information to your organisation. Such people need to be seen as *information gatherers* in addition to their 'official' role. For too long their knowledge has been neglected; organisations have begun to realise its value as they put the customer at the *top* of the organisation chart. But information is generated by *every individual* and all parts of the organisation; new experiences happen every day; new lessons learned for the benefit of colleagues elsewhere. The Learning Organisation has members who recognise that learning is not just about 'me and my skills', but is also about 'the information I receive daily and what I do with it'.

Nancy Dixon's second step is about *integrating information*. There have to be means of recording and sharing, and here information technology can help enormously. What is relevant to a particular matter has to be sifted and collected. We know how powerful information is, and individuals or teams may well wish to withhold, interpret, filter, summarise or delay it. (Averaging, consolidating and summarising are great enemies of the Learning Organisation and have caused many wrong decisions to be made in businesses over the years.) Data relevant to a particular process or customer revenue stream may be generated by quite different units, separated by organisational boundaries. 'Horizontal' organisations clearly encourage integrated information flows. Flat and team-based organisations which are connected through shared databases help also, provided that hierarchical and boundary games are not being played.

If organisational boundaries do get in the way then we need what Dixon calls 'boundary-spanning people'. Their role is to collate and then distribute information across boundaries, and to facilitate shared understanding. There may be a need to *understand* what information from 'across the water' means (financial or technical data for example), or the need may just be to receive it. This leads us to the third step in the cycle, *interpretation*.

Boards of companies are a classic example here of people presented with integrated information being asked to make meaning from it and draw conclusions as to action. Inevitably, since most information has various interpretations, judgement is as strong a factor as analysis. The Learning Organisation needs to concern itself with one question:

> For each critical process serving the customers of this organisation, do we have satisfactory collective mechanisms for the collation, distribution, and interpretation of

relevant information that will keep everybody working
with that process in touch with customer requirements?

This is not 'the manager's job' in a hierarchical sense. There
must be a process that involves all those with a contribution,
and a supportive culture that allows open discussion, questioning and interpretation.

The final stage in Dixon's cycle is about the *authority to act*
on the interpretation. Here the philosophy of empowerment to
the lowest levels acts for and against us. It asks individuals to
use their *own* interpretation to take appropriate action. There
is no doubt that in roles very close to customers this is
frequently the right approach. However, there comes a point
in the complexity of a problem where a *collective interpretation*
is going to yield a better decision. One of the skills of today's
leadership is to define the lines of decision-making authority.

Sharing best practice

Sharing best practice goes beyond information that is directly
customer-related. What have we discovered about organisational
models? Who has experimented with human asset accounting?
Where have we been most successful in the development of
minority groups? How has the division gaining the top quality
award managed this achievement? Which unit has just nego-
tiated a new kind of alliance with another organisation? The
issue is to create effective 'organisational dialogues' where
experience as well as knowledge is shared.

The answers are not 'rocket science'. In our unit in ICL we
pass on experience through electronic newsletters entitled
'Learning Matters', and have 'Organisational Learning Days'
to share experiences. The Learning Organisation recognises
the need, and individuals take the responsibility, to set up
mechanisms that work and that achieve credibility and value.
The 'work family' or 'community' concept discussed when we
looked at teams in Chapter 7 is a useful concept for thinking
about such sharing – groups of people with a common interest.

Figure 8.2
Knowledge-sharing across 'learning generations'

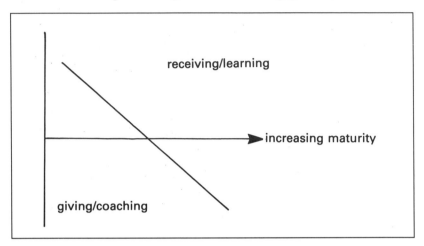

'Learning generations'

Most mature organisations are made up of different generations of maturity. It is always wrong to talk in terms of age
bands, because people's capacity to learn varies so much and
we do not want anybody to feel they do not have to be
continuously learning. Broadly speaking however, the younger
generation are doing more *receiving* than *giving*. The good
news about them is that they do not have too much *unlearning*
to do, and are freshly receptive. They can be powerful forces
for change in the Learning Organisation, if their voice and
actions are encouraged. The reverse would be true of the older
generation, but an important role for them is to be sharing
their knowledge and experience with others. This is illustrated
in Figure 8.2.

This involves the skills of coaching and mentoring, which
should be well developed in the Learning Organisation. Thus
we believe it is important for groups such as new graduate
entrants to have older mentors who 'hold the map' of the
organisation to guide and help them in their learning. Such

mentors need to be role-model learners themselves, not merely passers-on of the past.

POWERPOINT

Does your organisation have, for each customer-centred process, ways of collating and distributing information collected at all levels, and for its collective interpretation?

Does your organisation have a variety of mechanisms for sharing best practice in every area of the organisation's activities?

Is it normal in your organisation for younger people to have personal mentors and guides to help them with their learning about the organisation, how it functions, and how to achieve their goals?

Benchmarking

The days when people laughed at strange visitors from a company called Honda visiting the Manx TT races and photographing the bikes from every angle have long gone. Those were the people who learnt so much from competitors that they eventually destroyed them. Yet the concept of *seriously* understanding what others were doing as a means of setting some stretching targets to keep ahead of the game is relatively new to Western organisations. The classic model was pioneered by Xerox Corporation, who in 1979 became sufficiently threatened by Canon invading the market that they had so richly enjoyed for many years that they set up one of the most thorough product-benchmarking exercises in history. It paid off for them, and they began recovering the share they had been losing. Today they are a leading proponent of benchmarking methodology. What started as engineering and product quality comparisons now extends to all management processes. More recently, a 1993 report in the UK by Coopers and Lybrand claimed that 67 per cent of the Times

1000 Companies were using benchmarking, and it had major interest from top management.

Rank Xerox define benchmarking as:

> A continuous systematic process of evaluating companies recognised as industry leaders, to determine business and work processes that represent 'best practices' *and* establish rational performance goals.

There are many other similar definitions. David Saxl, an independent consultant in this area, uses the

> continuous, systematic search for an implementation of best practices which lead to superior performance.

The formal benchmarking process consists of:

Planning → Analysis → Integration → Action → Maturity

Planning – the subject, the organisations, the methodology. Subjects may be many and varied, from products (where it all started) to services, processes, culture, policies and results. Methods may include special external studies, conferences, databases, literature, exhibitions, and deliberate collaboration between interested parties.

The choice of benchmarking targets will depend on the subject. It could be for example competitors, opinion leaders, best-practice organisations, or other clusters. Clearly the preservation of good relationships is an important key to success, since for maximum benefit an organisation wants to repeat the cycle.

Analysis – the measurement of the gap in performance, and if possible the *anticipated* future gap.

Integration – this is the synthesis of the data obtained into the definition of goals for improvement, and building those goals into the planning processes of the organisation.

Action – implementation and measurement of progress towards the goals set.

Maturity – assessing whether we have achieved a leadership position (or whatever was the goal) and to what extent the process of benchmarking is firmly integrated into our management system.

This does not involve looking at *competitors* only, but at 'best-in-class' organisations as well. If a company falls into both categories they definitely need to be understood! Of course one studies and evaluates competitive strategies, activities, products and services as a means of shaping or reshaping one's own. It is best to do this through going to customers or using what is in the public domain – either purchasable or in print.

Internal benchmarking is important and relatively easy to implement. The question is: 'who is best and why in *our* group?' This is of value in encouraging learning from one another within the organisation, but is limited to the best practice existing internally.

Functional and process benchmarking is where specific functions or processes are compared with the best in the organisational sector, and in general. Competitors can be included here, as the benchmarking data may not be directly of commercial advantage.

Organisations who have travelled the road for longer than others report some of the lessons learnt. These include:

- the need for training and discipline in systematic methodology
- the integration into other initiatives concerned with quality and process, and especially into planning
- turning analysis into action
- the need to be selective rather than benchmark everything in sight.

Benchmarking is a prime learning experience for those involved; the key is to make the transfer to organisational change. Obtaining thorough information is one thing; but translating it into real action is another. The natural resistance summed up by the 'Not-Invented-Here' attitude applies less to external best practice than to internal, but it is still there. So the changing of behaviour that constitutes the real learning requires determined effort and senior sponsorship for success.

Benchmarking learning itself

This is an important aspect of benchmarking. The aim of this book is to provide a means of assessing where you are along the road towards the true Learning Organisation. But what specific measures are available to share with other organisations?

We would strongly recommend benchmarking the Learning Organisation as a whole, using an approach such as our 'Powerpoints', rather than the more typical metrics of:

- total training spend
- training spend/employee
- training spend/revenue
- training spend/paycost
- days training per employee.

We were asked by a journalist recently about training days per person, and responded that we preferred to talk about learning rather than training. 'How many learning days per year then?' he asked. Naturally, we replied '365'! Nonetheless, we do need to use easily available data, however questionable it may be as a full indicator. A major survey we conducted in the information technology industry in 1993 showed typical figures of 3–7 per cent of paycost (equivalent to 7–17 days per person) and 1–2 per cent of revenues. Organisations depending primarily on service revenues and scarce skills need to spend more, and it is only meaningful to make comparisons with organisations that have similar employee profiles.

Another application might be in the context of competencies.

Thus we might want to answer the question: 'Do our international project managers have the right profile of knowledge and skills for our purposes?'

Traditionally, consultants might have come in and done an internal exercise to examine the skills and capabilities of the best project managers as perceived by the organisation. But how do we know if ours are really competitive? The benchmarking approach would pick 10–15 organisations with a good reputation, carry out appropriate interviews with line managers and high-performing project managers, and analyse accordingly. Asking customers what they think is *always* a good idea.

Organisations find it helpful to share information on *employee opinion surveys*. There are various groupings in the UK and Continental Europe who share results on a core set of about 20 questions. Not only is this a way of measuring change management progress, but it is a useful way of benchmarking some key parameters of the Learning Organisation, such as perceptions of commitment to learning, and effectiveness of 'learning planning' processes.

Likewise most organisations would commission either internally or externally from suitable agencies surveys of *customer satisfaction* or *customer care*. In some industry sectors independent agencies produce league tables, which are taken very seriously. The question for the Learning Organisation is not 'are you satisfied with your position in the league?' but 'what does this tell me about my need to improve?'. Are you *defensive* or *responsive*? The same applies to your customer relations departments. Is the goal to deal with complaints and leave the customer feeling OK? That is worthy, but the higher goal is to see the learning opportunities from what has gone wrong. One of us made a suggestion to a large airline that we felt would increase its competitive service advantage, but the staff seemed unequipped to deal with correspondence that was actually helpful. The airline sent back a letter steeped in public relations hype. We phoned and asked, 'But what about our idea then?' 'Oh,' came the reply, 'we've passed that to another department, and that's the end of our responsibility.'

European quality model

The European Foundation for Quality Management (EFQM) was formed in 1988 by 14 leading European businesses, and in 1992 launched the European Quality Model based on nine parameters of a 'Total Quality Organisation'. The model is designed to encourage business excellence, and has factors split into 'enablers' (*how*) and 'results' (*what*). Organisations are encouraged to pursue self-assessment against the listed criteria for each parameter. Sets of questions are suggested against each criterion.

When organisations consider themselves ready to apply for an award, a written submission is made which is then assessed by trained assessors. Distinguished individuals act as jurors and may request site visits by assessors; their findings lead to the jurors' final recommendations. The percentages (or weightings) shown in Figure 8.3 were derived from extensive consultation, but organisations are allowed to use different weightings if they think they are justified.

There are many attractions in the use of the European Quality Model. It reinforces the 'balanced score-card' approach to business (see page 8). Some consortiums have been created to enable sharing of self-assessment methodologies; one such comprises Eastman Kodak, Lucas Management Systems, British Telecom, Northern Telecom, ICL, Royal Mail, and the Trustee Savings Bank. In their report of February 1994, this consortium highlighted the benefits of a systematic, cyclic framework that balances business results with the processes that lead to them. According to Northern Telecom, the framework is beneficial because it:

- enables benchmarking against a 'world standard'
- measures effectiveness of improvements implemented
- covers all aspects of the business
- provides a challenge to spur continuous improvement
- measures today's status and identifies opportunities for improvement

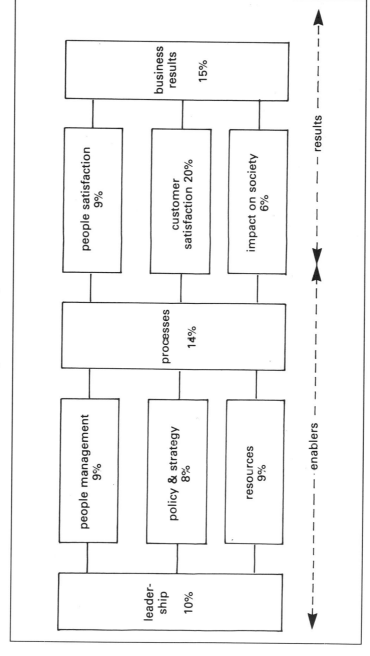

Figure 8.3
European Quality Model

- builds team spirit by involving everyone in an honest, non-threatening environment.

Although this framework highlights continuous improvement, we would like to see more explicit emphasis on learning processes as a route to excellence.

The recommended methods of scoring the enablers and the results are described in the tables below.

SCORING THE ENABLERS

Approach		Deployment
Role model for other organisations	100%	Applied to full potential in all areas
Clear evidence of systematic preventative approach	75%	Applied to 75% of organisation
Regular review, integrated with business	50%	Applied to 50% to organisation
Sound approach, occasional review	25%	Applied to 25% of organisation
Anecdotal evidence only	0%	Little effective usage

SCORING THE RESULTS

Result		Scope
Excellent results, best in class	100%	All areas addressed
Most results better than benchmarks	75%	Most areas addressed
Positive trends over three years; benchmarks used	50%	Many areas addressed
Some positive trends, compares well with target	25%	Some areas addressed
Anecdotal evidence only	0%	Few areas addressed

From the point of view of the Learning Organisation such models and self-assessment are powerfully helpful. They encourage continuous learning from others in order to become 'best of the best' as well as cross-boundary learning as units compete for the best assessments and the coveted EFQM award. The trained assessors are themselves influences for learning. It is a significantly better application of effort than that required by the bureaucratic ISO9000 (BS5750 in the UK) standard.

 **POWERPOINT**

Is there a systematic benchmarking methodology operated consistently throughout your organisation?

Does it include internal, competitive, functional and process benchmarks?

Is there senior sponsorship and programme management?

Is it built into the expectations of every department, team and individual that learning from benchmarking is a *normal* way of life, and are achievement targets regularly reset as a result?

Are there specific benchmarks relating to learning?

Mergers, acquisitions and alliances

The competitive pressures acting on organisations today require more complex and more cross-border *alliances* than ever before. The acquisition mania of the 1980s has given way to a greater focus on alliances, even within defined boundaries between competitors. Thus ICL, Bull and Siemens Nixdorf, fierce competitors in the market-place, collaborate together in research on advanced computing at the European Centre for Research in Computing in Munich. It is quite likely that Europe will see families of partnerships emerging, along the Japanese *keiretsu* principle, who trade between one another and support one another on common fronts. For the champions of the Learning Organisation this is potentially good news, if the opportunities can be harnessed.

It is a well-researched fact that the majority of mergers and acquisitions fail against their original objectives – which are usually put together by finance and legal departments. They fail because people-related issues have not been taken properly into account. This may have something to do with key players and their motivation, with cultural differences of many kinds, with incompatibility between business processes, or with loss of customer confidence.

The rationale for an acquisition may well be linked to learning, that is to gain access to technology, markets, or expertise of one kind or another. More commonly it is to reduce competition, grow the organisation's revenue and assets, gain a more efficient cost-base, and so on. In our experience, legal 'due diligence' procedures rarely check out how and where knowledge and experience are held – they focus on the more tangible accounting assets. They may make an inventory of the senior people, but usually with the objective of understanding the cash liabilities if they leave. The loss of accumulated learning could be much more devastating.

As two organisations' accumulated learning becomes available to each other, the benefits should be tremendous. They should take the best of each other's processes; share all their commercial and technical knowledge; and plan a future which exploits their combined skills.

Too often, however, suspicion and distrust permeate. The purchaser dominates and forces change in line with its view of the world; 'information being power', it is not shared but kept close to the chest for as long as possible; relationships and teams of many years' standing are broken up; and people drift away from the new organisation. It is not surprising that many fail when the learning of the acquired party is not respected and safeguarded. 'After all,' people say, 'who values the results of *our* efforts any more?' As we shall discuss in Chapter

9 the premium that is paid for the 'intangible' assets may be frittered away as those assets cease to have productive value.

In an *alliance*, or genuine merger, depending on the structure of ownership it is more likely that learning will be shared because the rationale for the union will be based on both parties having something to gain. Even so, the full availability of learning is rarely stated explicitly, as financial figures and market shares dominate discussions without consideration of the vital *how* they are going to be achieved.

The Learning Organisation that sees the significance of the learning gains will ensure that an assessment is made of the proposed partner or acquisition in terms of their strength as a Learning Organisation in their own right. All the 'Powerpoints' in this book should serve as checkpoints in that assessment, together with an evaluation of how the constituent organisations can be merged synergistically.

 POWERPOINT

Does your organisation have a check-list for 'due diligence' to be made in cases of mergers, acquisitions or alliances, which enables assessment of the proposed partner against the characteristics of a Learning Organisation?

Does your organisation have a systematic approach to respecting *and* absorbing/disseminating the accumulated learning of the new partner?

Would your organisation be prepared to reorient its strategy, structure, systems and culture as a result of the new partnership?

Adapting to change in the environment

The Learning Organisation is characterised by being nimble in adapting to changes in its environment. Individuals often perceive what is happening, may even make presentations or write about it, but does the organisation take any notice? The answer lies in four factors:

- How *efficient* are the collection, distribution and interpretation of information relating to the market and the environment?
- How *open-minded* are senior managers in formulating scenarios for the future and deciding on a strategy?
- How *supportive* is the culture for deciding on a change of direction and implementing it?
- How *fast* is this all able to happen?

Anglo-Dutch Shell is the oft-quoted example of the organisation that regularly reviews different future scenarios, as described in Peter Schwartz's book *The Art of the Long View*. As a result they were strategically prepared for a sudden drop in the oil price in the early 1970s, and for the collapse of the Russian Empire in 1990. One is dependent on the willingness of key individuals to have an open mind and to change direction, responding to new situations.

But is the prophet honoured in his or her own country? Or are unpopular predictions swept into the filing cabinet because we lack the muscle to grasp what might be very uncomfortable? The consistent institutionalisation of processes that examine trends, such as Shell's, clearly help *as long as they have credibility with the key managers*. That is not easily won – 'we're in the swamp up to our necks in alligators, while these HQ types swan off to conferences and think about futures that will never arrive if we don't get our act together this quarter' may be the type of response. The solution lies in involving the key managers in the collective learning that is necessary.

Many models and mechanisms for strategy development are available. Perhaps the best-known, and widely useful, is the analysis of Strengths, Weaknesses, Opportunities and Threats (SWOT) as a means of assessing the starting-point. A question mark hangs over the extent to which it is realistic to set long-term goals in today's world, but organisations do need a sense of vision that gives direction. Bob Garratt describes his methodology for helping organisations with managing change in his book *Creating a Learning Organisation*. He recommends analyses of this kind leading to projects 'crucial for survival' composed of *volunteers* who see the development opportunities for themselves.

The chief executive, or comparable leader, plays the most significant role here in his or her *stimulation* of thinking, evaluation and change. The history of organisations is written around such key men and women who did, or did not, see the need for change at the right time.

Strategy as a learning process

Evaluating strategic direction, working through the milestones of success and assessing the needed resources are a key process for organisations. The process of strategic planning, which requires understanding and interpreting large quantities of information, should not be left to a few boffins in the business development department. Those that need to carry out the strategies have to have been involved in their development. If one is *told* what to do, one inevitably interprets according to one's understanding. Strategic planning provides a means of sharing in the same direction, through having potential differences and conflicts out on the table, and focusing towards agreement. Aids to doing this may be very simple, like the popular 'metaplanning' brainstorming technique which uses 'Post-its' and coloured stickers to enable voting and prioritising. Swieringa and Wierdsma describe a Learning Organisation as being less a 'tourist', ie one that has a defined endpoint and works out how to get there, but more a 'trekker' – that is, *it sets a direction, acts and achieves some experience, and then maybe resets the direction*. The focus is on 'learning through doing'

Figure 8.4
The 'sigmoid curve'

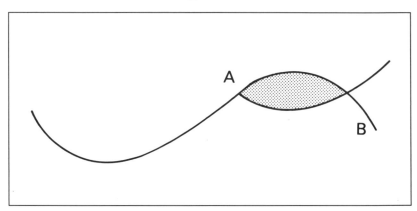

rather than analytical conclusions as to directions. This is pragmatic, but also responsive to the speed of changes that hit us.

Charles Handy devotes a chapter of his *The Empty Raincoat* to discussion of the 'sigmoid curve' – 'the story of life itself'. The secret is to recognise that everything has a cycle and to see what the next curve should be at point 'A' rather than point 'B'. The problem is that at point 'A' all the messages may reinforce the continuation of the rising curve. (See Figure 8.4.)

There are many examples of organisations that have been successful and yet failed to adapt at critical times, and – good news – of those who have failed and then recovered through intensive learning and internal change. Advances in technology are perhaps the most potent driver of change today, and have hit the pioneers of their own industry in a most unforgiving way. The business of information technology has caused not only many flowers to bloom, but proud giants to stumble. For IBM, Digital and other major corporations it involved a radical rethink of their core strategies, structure and values. Slowly the manufacturers are turning themselves into service providers, and it is a measure of the learning capability of the talent they have that so few have actually fallen by the wayside.

POWERPOINT

Does your organisation have a credible process for examining the external trends that affect its business?

Is there a mechanism for sharing such findings amongst key influencers and learning together about the implications for change?

Is strategic planning carried out as a shared learning experience?

The power of learning (and unlearning) together

To quote Swieringa and Wierdsma once again, 'organisational learning means the changing of organisational behaviour. Individual learning is a *necessary* but not a *sufficient* condition for organisational learning. *Mutual* behaviour change requires mutual learning.' Thinking things through, understanding the environment and its changes, taking action *together* are going to be much more effective than piecemeal learning by individuals. Organisations lose an immense amount of momentum and energy through not understanding when collective learning is needed. For example, the success of change management is dependent on all those who need to be part of the change understanding for themselves why the change is needed, and working out together what has to be done. Communication is not a substitute for 'education', which is the reorientation of both hearts *and* minds towards new directions.

All organisations have the need for more attention to the constant questioning and resetting of assumptions – going beyond 'pragmatic adjustments'. Such learning needs to be met collectively. Organisations find this difficult, as it involves a lot of *unlearning* and consequent discomfort. Asking third parties to prescribe fundamental organisational change – often because the organisational political agendas cannot be faced – is never a substitute for dealing with the issues together, owning the intellectual needs together, and then acting together.

Courage is needed. When the framework is reset, all the diversity of individuals and their learning capabilities can be harnessed towards the common goals.

We would expect a lot more collective learning to be taking place in the Learning Organisation. This takes place in work teams both formally and informally, but in dispersed and informal structures it is needed in the following kinds of situation:

- understanding changes in the environment which affect everyone in the organisation (education)
- cross-boundary problem-solving (action learning)
- specific knowledge and skill shifts (capability enhancement).

Education

There is a place for an individual attending the classic business school event, but it is not what many professors think it is. Many such programmes concentrate on providing *solutions*, derived mostly from the experience of other organisations, rather than learning through *problem-solving*. As a learning experience, such events are not so much, we would suggest, about the content as:

- an opportunity to benchmark externally
- an opportunity for time to think
- an opportunity to create a network outside the normal environment in which one works.

The choice therefore of one event against another would be made on the structure rather than the syllabus, so that these dimensions can be maximised. Would we expect dynamic change in the way a person carries out his or her role as a result? That would be unrealistic. One of the weaknesses of traditional 'one-off' attendance at management education events is that having a number of managers who become individually more skilled does not lead to having a more skilled management team. Indeed the conscientious evaluator of management programmes frequently finds that the individual is very aware of their personal learning, but the environment in which they operate is basically unchanged, and therefore their ability to apply what they have learnt is restricted. The reabsorption into the pressures of the role back in the organisation soon dilutes the memory, and at best only some actions may be taken that are formed as a result of reflection during the event. As for transfer of that learning to others, even if a formally organised briefing event is held, the *internalisation* of the experience is for the individual who attended only. Unless the individual manager is able to apply it in such a way that the environment itself changes, then the organisation's behaviour does not change and it does not itself learn.

A special case concerns the chief executive (or equivalent) with the power directly to influence the organisation, or a part of it, in its entirety. He or she *is* able to change the environment, and there are many examples of such people who have 'changed their world'. Even so, they will only do it by taking the hearts and minds of their team with them, and that may require a collective learning experience.

The same observations apply to traditional management education in general where the premiss is one of experts providing solutions, rather than learning from problems. Although organisations continue to support such events both internally and externally, the voice of the critics is growing significantly. Alan Mumford, a frequent proponent of action-based learning, suggested in a 1993 article that the following questions should be asked:

- Do designers have a theory of managerial learning which they are applying through their work?
- Do they have a structured practice of monitoring the impact of this theory on the design and on the achievements of the offered learning experience?

- Do they give appropriate attention not just to what individuals are learning but *how* they learn it?

His researches show that formal systems of development have had much less effect than the designers hoped for. Mumford recommends three ways of improving performance for both individual and collective learning:

- improved design of learning experiences
- increased recognition of opportunities to learn through normal work experiences
- helping managers 'learning how to learn'.

Does this mean that executive education is a waste of time and money? Sometimes it is – if it is piecemeal and individualised. But the potential in learning *together* is still enormous. For either a working team or a cross-boundary group, being exposed to issues and problems together, and thinking through the implications together, is powerful. We are strong believers in the facilitated event, bringing in inputs of knowledge and experience as appropriate, and learning together what it all means. In a fast-changing environment this should happen on a regular basis – two or three times a year – where the sole objective is to recalibrate the understanding of the world. This may result in a number of team tasks being formulated that apply, explore, and evaluate aspects of what has been learnt – for sharing at the next gathering. We certainly support Alan Mumford also in taking time out to understand the effective *processes* of collective learning – in order to become more efficient at it.

This is not the same as the 'customised' business school programme. We are referring to events driven from need and designed for the team members. At the executive level it removes any feelings of isolation, of feeling that one is a 'lone voice in the wilderness'. It breaks down the tendency to regard the 'company' as some impersonal controlling body, and changes the 'them and us' syndrome to just 'us'. For people meeting together from different parts of the organisation, the advantages in cross-boundary learning and understanding are clear. This is not about sorting out *conflicts*, but sharing in learning together.

Some parts of ICL experimented with an exposure of people at all levels and with many kinds of roles to this 'learning from the environment', starting with direct contact with customers' needs and perceptions. Called 'Discovery' programmes, they have comprised a series of events enabling redefinition of roles and capabilities in self-managed learning teams.

Collective problem-solving

Since learning from experience is so powerful, we need to ask how this may be exploited beyond the working team level. There will be no universal solutions here, but the principle is *deliberately* to seek opportunities for cross-boundary problem-solving. This may be part of a planned development programme, such as the 'action learning'-oriented MBA programmes pioneered by the University of Buckingham in the UK, or internally set-up 'self-managed learning' groups that we discussed in Chapter 6. The new devolved and flexible organisational structures provide many emerging opportunities – the question is how these opportunities get utilised. If there was a 'director of knowledge management', as we recommend in our final chapter, one of his or her accountabilities might be to look for such opportunities and set up project groups.

Capability enhancement

There will always be new knowledge, and sometimes new skills, that everybody needs to learn. Wherever possible this should be done in working teams so that the learning continues through mutual practical application. Team members are likely to be at more or less the same level of competence, and can improve together by helping each other. For example, if the team needs to learn how to evaluate and manage their business on the basis of shareholder value, all members need to know how to be able to do it at the same time. Otherwise the application of the learning will be less effective for the organisation.

 **POWERPOINT**

Does your organisation ensure that regular 'educational' events take place for appropriate groups *across* the organisation's internal boundaries?

Does your organisation look for opportunities for collective problem-solving?

Does your organisation hold events for learning new capabilities *together*?

Pointers for action

What marks out the effectiveness of a total Learning Organisation from those that are just good at helping the learning of individuals is the ability to share and transfer that learning for the good of all, and to understand how and when learning *together* is critically important. Organisational structures, and many new models being experiemented with, have an important influence on the effectiveness of total learning. The relationship with the external world is a key part of organisational learning.

This is the most difficult aspect of the Learning Organisation to make effective and keep that way. As recommended earlier, a senior executive taking responsibility for collective learning and knowledge-sharing is essential to hold things together. Other lines of action you might consider are:

- to examine structures carefully from the point of view of maximising learning at individual, team and organisational levels

- when structures are determined, to ensure dialogue mechanisms are set up and work across the boundaries
- to set up a benchmarking programme and ensure that the results are turned into action goals
- to set up a Learning Organisation due-diligence check-list for mergers and acquisitions
- to consider where a collective learning programme could help the sharing of knowledge and experience eg in the formulation of strategy, and develop a pilot approach.

The organisation that achieves all we have discussed in this chapter will be very high up on the continuum of Learning Organisations.

9

The Power of Valuing Learning

Enhancing the measures of success

In Chapter 1 we listed measures of success and argued that the Learning Organisation should undoubtedly lead to improvements in the full range of these measures. We would expect to see the benefits that we described for customers, employees and shareholders realised, as well as improvements on every chosen measure through the effective application of all we have discussed.

ICL uses a four-level evaluation system of learning programmes in the formal sense:

Level 1: programme satisfaction (where the programme may be a series of learning experiences)
Level 2: measurable increase in knowledge, skills, attitudes or experience
Level 3: measurable impact and application in the individual's role
Level 4: measurable impact on the organisation's objectives.

The last level is one that causes much difficulty. To come to qualitative conclusions regarding links between specific learning and increased customer satisfaction, innovation, or image improvement (for example) can seem quite logical. The difficulty always is to relate investment to the 'bottom line'. We could argue that the *believer* in the Learning Organisation as a way of life does not need such proof. But it is instructive and powerful to think through the links that can be made.

What does it do for the bottom line?

If the Learning Organisation is about competitive success, we should expect it to affect the financial results not specifically for this quarter but on a continuing basis. Every person responsible for a profit or surplus line should understand that the focus on continuous organisational and individual learning is *essential* for both today's *and* tomorrow's results.

The profit and loss account

The problem with the aspects discussed below is that rarely are they overtly visible, and we do not find it comfortable to look for *invisible* costs and *lost* revenues. They are there nonetheless.

Revenues

These revenue advantages may not all come immediately – few investments yield their return in the first year. We are talking about the continuous generation of fresh revenues as a direct result of effective organisational learning. They may come from:

- *learning about what is happening in the market-place and in the environment, and being able to respond speedily through bringing more innovative products and services to the market faster than others.* The proverbial frog that was being boiled slowly never saw his demise coming. The Learning Organisation moves faster than competitors in changing directions to meet new opportunities. We mentioned this in Chapter 1 as a benefit to customers, but it is clearly the source of continuing and future revenues.
- *having the skills that can provide what customers want to buy.* People buy from people, not from organisations. In a service-based organisation, the available skills make or break the business opportunities. The traditional 'pro-

fessions' have known this for a long time, and compete strongly to get the best people, grow them and keep them. Today, manufacturing and distribution organisations know also that their competitive advantage comes from being *smarter* rather than bigger. Contracts can be won or lost on the confidence that customers have in the 'ability to deliver' of the supplier. Organisations should look seriously at any contracts lost due to lack of skills, in order to set in motion the right plan for acquiring the necessary capability.

- *benchmarking against competition; learning how to exploit their weaknesses and the available market niches*. The West learnt this from the Japanese, but some sectors are applying Western systemisation to it and being very effective. Xerox would undoubtedly attribute its fight back against Canon to its mastery of these techniques, and is today a role model in benchmarking.

- *understanding and responding to customers' needs and expectations*. Everybody would claim to have 'customer care' as a key value today (though it is not always obvious to their customers!). But it is one thing to have the programmes and the data, and another to mobilise the organisation to respond in a co-ordinated and dedicated way. Lost customers are hard to recover, and one bad story repeated to 10 friends can leave an indelible negative impact of the organisation. Recovering that lost revenue takes much cost and effort.

- *learning how to exploit previous successes and avoid repeating previous failures*. This is the essence of organisational learning, and one of the easiest ways to influence the revenue line. We described in Chapter 8 the skill of management consultancy McKinsey's in building up their store of knowledge and experience (see pages 120–1). People like to buy from *experienced* suppliers. 'Reference sells', which tell the customer that you have been there before and already learnt some of the potential problems in your product or service, are very powerful in giving confidence to a buyer.

*Note – it is often easier to estimate the lost revenues from **not** being able to do the above as you observe opportunities lost.*

Costs

Most of the costs from being ineffective as a Learning Organisation will be due to *wasted people-time*, the great invisible cost of organisations that is rarely measured. However, there are other costs due to mistakes, ignorance, and personal agendas which lead to wasted expenditures on every cost line.

Some of the costs that can be avoided arise from:

- *duplicating the same work in different parts of the organisation*. Duplication happens because parts of the organisation do not know or do not *want* to know whether others have solved problems before, or are working on them.
- *making the same mistakes as before because the lessons learnt were never translated into the organisation's inventory of 'wisdom' and made available*. Organisations do make expensive mistakes. Those, for example, who are involved in large contract bids and their management have learnt to their cost how important risk and resource management are. If they were not able to learn from these experiences, and generate some accepted disciplines and methodologies from them, the risk of repeating errors is enormous.
- *solving the same problems more than once*. This arises from not having the means or motivation to discover who might have experienced and solved a problem before. So people spend time and money 're-inventing wheels'. One of the risks of the devolved organisation which does not have sharing mechanisms is that this becomes an epidemic.
- *being locked into inappropriate processes and not being able to 'unlearn' old ways of doing things*. Killing well-established bureaucratic systems is amazingly hard, especially when it strikes at the power base of individuals and departments. Bureaucracy has many costs, mostly in the quite unnecessary expenditure of time.

- *concentrating on internal problems and arguments instead of focusing on customers and their care.* We mentioned this above, but this is more than just being unresponsive to customers' needs. It is an affliction that so easily besets organisations, especially amongst senior management, and results in internal negotiations of various kinds taking more time and energy than external ones.
- *power games and political agendas gaining precedence over what is right for the organisation as a whole; unwillingness to share knowledge across the organisation.* Power games and politics are always with us. They cost money, mostly invisible, in the choices and decisions that individuals and teams make when their own motivation is uppermost. A Learning Organisation, however, tries to set up a communications and cultural environment where political agendas are exposed and dealt with constructively, and where knowledge is made available and accessible to all.
- *spending on 'rationalisation' by paying people to leave the organisation, when forethought on retraining them in new skills would have prevented both this cost and the hiring of the needed skill.* Many managers are very impatient. The necessity to 'get the cost-base down' leads to the need for reductions in headcount, and a 'programme' (which today might include a lot of counselling help for individuals) will be devised to achieve the necessary. Asking the right questions sufficiently in advance regarding the capability to learn new skills, or the identification of needs in other parts of the organisation, are often not done. No wonder some organisations have set up their own 'internal outplacement' resources – which pay for themselves many times over – to ensure the right questions are asked and diagnostics used.
- *spending on training and education without thinking systematically about the learning benefits or the alternative solutions.* Many organisations proudly display their expenditure on training, as measured by the costs of the training department and people going on courses. This does not make a Learning Organisation, and we question the effectiveness of much

systematised training as against more experiential ways of learning. The evaluation of training against its learning objectives is still a discipline many find hard to follow.

- *lost productivity and long learning curves in times of change.* This may be either organisational, team or individual, and is so important that we discuss it in more depth below. This arises from poor management of change, be it a poorly-planned individual induction programme, or dealing with an organisational or structural change. Relevant learning needs should be systematically planned for.
- *spending the organisation's money inappropriately through lack of knowledge, skills, experience or appropriate attitudes.* Spending through ignorance is rarely calculated, perhaps because it is potentially embarassing. It happens in areas of making wrong purchasing choices, asking consultants to tell us what another part of the organisation already knows, making cross-border ventures without necessary research and falling foul of legal or cultural pitfalls, and so on. Of course, we regard every mistake as a learning opportunity, but they can be expensive.
- *not encouraging continuous innovation from all employees to reduce costs and increase efficiency.* Money is actually spent by employees at all levels. As people who should understand the value of their part of the business, and have some ownership of it, they should be rewarded – if only psychologically – for improvements. We may be surprised at the results.
- *people not being encouraged to take ownership of their learning, and waiting for things to be done for them.* It happens sometimes that agreement is reached that a learning plan should be followed, and a year later nothing has been achieved. This is often because we have regarded the manager as the one who should take the initiative. The cost is in the level of sub-optimal performance – which, summed up for all inviduals, may be substantial.

Note – it is worthwhile costing some of these when they arise, as

*they do frequently in most organisations, to remind ourselves of
what could have been avoided.*

 POWERPOINT

Does your organisation link revenue plans to the capability that is
needed to achieve them?

Does your organisation examine lost revenues and relate them to
lack of knowledge, skills, attitudes or experience in individuals, *or*
to ineffective organisational use of those?

Can your organisation assess and talk about costs arising from
aspects of ineffectiveness as a Learning Organisation?

Does your organisation look for and quantify costs arising from
unnecessary duplication and overlap?

The 'balance sheet' – organisational health check

The 'balance sheet' is about the state of health of a business,
and indicates its present and future viability. *Assets* typically
include fixed assets such as plant and buildings, and liquid
assets such as debtors and bank balances. Unfortunately, the
problem of finding a satisfactory method of *human asset
accounting* has never been solved. We can regard human
resources as a largely variable cost on the profit and loss
account, and indeed the expenditure incurred in paying for
them appears there. At the same time, we can regard them as
an asset that appreciates with experience and investment in
continuing learning.

Can these assets be valued? They may be a significant
competitive advantage, especially if specialised and scarce.
Capitalising 'non-tangible' assets is a constant difficulty. Information technology companies have to decide whether to
capitalise investments in software; if they do, they normally

depreciate each year's investment over a period. Should 'brands' be capitalised, as the food and drinks company Grand Metropolitan suddenly decided to do in the late 1980s? Should the same be done for training investment? The problem with this is that it is very difficult to relate particular revenue streams to a particular investment, and indeed much training spend has little effect.

The best indicator of an *individual's* relative value is probably the gross remuneration they command as a full-time employee, or a proportion of their free-market value if they had to sell their capability. The latter is nearly always a higher sum compensating for the lack of continuous employment and the associated employment benefit packages. On the other hand, whether reflected in the remuneration paid or not, there may be a premium asset value arising from the specialised knowledge and experience that the person has of the organisation, its history and people; their ability to understand and work with the culture and the politics; or the 'intellectual property' value that they personally hold. How human assets are related to other assets is an unsolved accounting problem.

In *The Human Organisation – Its management and value* Rensis Likert attempted a system of human asset accounting which was actually put into practice in the R. G. Barry Corporation of Columbus, Ohio. A 'human capital balance sheet' was used where investments in 'replacements and development' were balanced with 'losses through attrition' and an amortisation based on expected future service. The basis was a cumulative historical cost asset valuation, ie recruitment plus development. The assumption was that if $x was invested in an individual's development, then his or her asset value increased by $x. Such an assumption does of course raise a number of questions as to the effectiveness of the development spend.

In a joint IPM/ICMA paper written in 1972, Giles and Robinson proposed the 'human asset multiplier'. This represents a number of years' capitalisation of annual remuneration. This is described in the following steps:

1. Distinguish the break-up value of the total assets and the values as 'a going concern'. The difference measures the value of the management and employees.
2. The human asset value should be less than or equal to the going concern value (say 7 × profits), less the net assets (due allowance being made for other goodwill elements).
3. Relate the result to the gross payroll to arrive at the average multiplier.
4. This is weighted for different categories of employees by assessing their personal value as part of the total asset value. The weighting, or multiplier, reflects:

qualifications/expertise	experience
attitudes	promotion capability
loyalty	replacement scarcity

and estimates of expected future service.

5. Apply the multiplier to gross remuneration.

In a case to which the method was applied, they evaluated the multipliers as:

senior mgt	2.5 +
middle mgt	1.5–3
supervisors	1–2
clerical/op	0–1.5

This approach also has its difficulties. It is very difficult to put relative values on the factors of personal value and estimates of future service. No accepted method has emerged as a standard. Occasionally we see a value being placed on individuals, such as football team transfers, or 'golden hello's' to attract people into corporations. Shares may rise or fall when key executives join or leave. For example, when the *Financial Times* reported in April 1994 that Ms Ann Iverson was leaving the post of chief executive of Mothercare to join an American organisation, the shares of the parent Storehouse fell by 4.8 per cent. Ms Iverson had turned round and revitalised the company, and was clearly viewed as a lost asset.

When does an asset become a liability?

Most fixed assets depreciate but do not normally become a liability, in the sense of having negative value. Human assets can become liabilities, however. Their knowledge and skills can depreciate in value and relevance with time, and although it is often recognised far too late, their 'portfolio' may have fallen behind the competitive levels.

Figure 9.1 shows another way to express the formula that the rate of learning needs to be greater than, or equal to, the rate

Figure 9.1
The importance of continuous learning

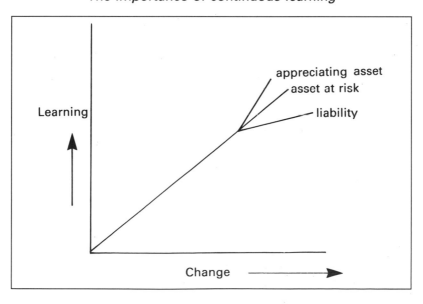

of change. If individuals, teams and organisations keep along, or above, the 45° line then they remain assets. However, once they fall below they run the risk of becoming a liability in that their skills become obsolete and there may no longer be a place for them. If termination has to be evoked the cost may be up to two or three years' salary depending on the country, the organisation's policies, and the person's years of service. There is a mutual role *and* interest here in the continuous benchmarking of an individual's capability profile against the needs of the organisation and its customers.

In some countries, for example Austria, the risk of redundancy payments is required by law to be shown on the balance sheet as an annual liability. Unfortunately there is no balancing asset figure! Obsolescence is not the only cause of losing people, of course, and we would expect the effective Learning Organisation to be minimising this through continuous learning for everybody. In rationalisation or downsizing exercises the need to reduce the cost-base sometimes means we lose more assets (especially the older ones with all the knowledge) than liabilities. The smart Learning Organisation is sufficiently flexible to reduce its running costs as necessary but at the same time maintain access to assets it has helped to grow. This may be through consultancy or subcontract arrangements, as shown in the UK by IBM's establishment of 'Skillbase'.

Here, as part of IBM's downsizing efforts, they set up a company in which they retained part-ownership (though this was later sold) and to which employees with saleable skills transferred. A level of consultancy work was guaranteed by IBM, declining over a period of time towards self-sufficiency for the individual.

The difficulties in putting numbers on our human assets should not deflect us from the principles involved. Even though a method may be imprecise, if we use it at differing periods it enables us to see the *trends* taking place. Thus, calculating 'shareholder value' and matching it against the asset value on the balance sheet on a regular basis is one way to track progress.

Let us think in more detail about the constituent components of the balance sheet and where the Learning Organisation can have an influence in terms of assets, goodwill and liabilities.

Assets

Our assets in this context are essentially people. We could argue that some of *the systems they create* become assets also – particularly (for example) information technology systems, competitive process engineering or reward systems. These may contribute to ouput just as much as an item of plant and machinery. Thus in information technology the software systems and networks are of much greater intrinsic value than the 'hardware' that may appear on the asset register. However, we risk making our case unnecessarily complex.

The Learning Organisation has people who:

- *continually grow their personal asset value of the knowledge, skill, attitudes and experience that are important to the organisation's success*. The value, or potential value, of the contribution that a person can make increases when one of these elements increases. This may be seen in improved performance in the job that is being done, or in the availability for broader or more responsible roles.
- *are motivated towards continual improvement of their own performance and consequently look for feedback from various sources, and use it constructively*. Some people do this naturally but a Learning Organisation encourages it in everyone – so that it is not just management worrying about asset appreciation.
- *are motivated towards looking for continuous improvements in everything they contribute to*. This includes improvements in revenues, costs, asset utilisation, customer satisfaction and goodwill.
- *are distinguished from people doing similar roles in other organisations by their skills, their role space, their initiative,*

the quality of their contribution and their motivation to succeed. We all know organisations where the people with whom one comes into contact are *different.* We remember the helpful receptionist, the guide who made our trip fun for us, the telephone operator who went to a lot of trouble to find somebody, the bus driver who thought our convenience more important than the strict route. They may not be perfect, but the difference is everything. They care about what they are doing, and about you as a customer. A *Financial Times* survey of business lounges in airports in June 1994 picked out Virgin Atlantic for having a deliberate atmosphere of *fun.*

Goodwill

Goodwill is defined as the premium between the *market value* and the *net asset value* according to the balance sheet. The value of human assets, of advantageous systems and processes, of brand image(s), and of 'intellectual property' may all be generally or specifically included. Quinn, in his book *Intelligent Enterprise*, quotes 'Tobin's Q' as the ratio of market value as a percentage of asset value. He quotes Tom Watson Jr of IBM as saying:

> All the value of this company is in its people. If you burned down all our plants, and we just kept our people and our information files, we would soon be as strong as ever. Take away our people and we might never recover.

This premium may be quite substantial. Quinn quotes some acquisitions in the USA between 1987 and 1990 with premiums from 55 to 1,720 per cent over the physical assets. These premia represent the value of people, databases, organisational capability, systems, alliances, and Intellectual Property Rights (IPRs).

The latter especially stem from learning and define 'products' in the knowledge sector. There are five legal categories: Patents, Registered Designs, Copyright, Trademarks and Service-marks. Owning the IPR gives an organisation the right to charge for its use by others through licensing. This applies for example to software, manufacturing processes, literature, and music, and the Rights can be traded as if they were a product or security. They represent a tangible output and value from an organisation's applied learning. The whole area is a legal nightmare, due to the difficulty in encapturing and describing the results of organisational learning that are clearly distinctive to that organisation. Some well-published court cases have included Xerox Corporation and Apple Computer over the use of icon-based user-interfaces – where the former claims the latter stole the concept from them. When highly valued people-assets move from one organisation to another, who owns what is in their head?

Liabilities

People may be liabilities as much as they are assets. The effective Learning Organisation does not need people who:

- have no interest in owning their continuous learning and performance improvement
- do not wish to share their own knowledge and experience
- are not prepared to spend personal time in helping others to learn
- are not prepared to think about their work content and make suggestions for improvement.

Such people will become 'yesterday's people' and, eventually, obsolete.

Poor structure, systems and cultural aspects of course can be liabilities also, and effectively produce 'negative goodwill'. For example:

- *restrictive controls and levels of authority that prevent people doing what they know is right (or experimenting); out-of-date processes that cause delays in decision-making, in bringing products and services to the market, and in solving customer problems.* Bureaucracy can be a stranglehold on flexibility, adaptability and speed of response. Good systems are important – can the organisation distinguish between those that *help* and those that *hinder*?
- *organisational structures that necessitate a lot of internal negotiation and rivalry over 'turf'.* Such situations not only divert energy towards internal rather than external issues, but cause information to be held as a weapon rather than shared openly. Thus learning decreases.
- *inadequate communication and information systems.* Poor communications, it has been said, are the cause of most things that go wrong in organisations. Freedom of information and the best possible efficient dissemination of it are the marks of the Learning Organisation.
- *reward systems that reward the wrong behaviours.* This is typified by various bonus schemes which encourage behaviours that no longer reflect the needs of the organisation.

One could undoubtedly list many other issues that become liabilities in the same sense.

There are people, systems and projects that show characteristics of both asset and liability. What we want to be sure of is that the net result is positive, ie an asset. It is useful to pause and draw up a specific balance sheet.

In the format suggested below, the two columns are filled on both positive and negative aspects, first with the *importance* of each item's effect, and second with its *strength*; these two are multiplied together and added up for all items on both sides. The summaries are then subtracted to give the overall balance. An example might be:

Area of Study: Quality Circles

Positive aspects	Imp	Strength	Negative aspects	Imp	Strength
involvement of all staff	8	8	routine that is losing momentum	8	5
value of improvements	9	6	circles used to focus on complaints	7	6
sharing of learning in circle	7	9	attendance levels fall off	9	5
cross-sharing between circles	6	5			
+ve		211	−ve		−127

On this basis we would conclude that Quality Circles continued to be an asset to the organisation.

 **POWERPOINT**

Does your organisation visibly treat people as assets and show concern that they are continually appreciating and not *depreciating*?

Does your organisation periodically and systematically assess its human liabilities?

Measuring a return for learning

One generalist way of looking at the contribution of learning which is aimed at performance improvement, whether for an *individual, a team, or an organisation*, is shown in Figure 9.2.

Learning programmes have a defined cost. Can we be as precise about the benefits?

Figure 9.2
Performance improvement

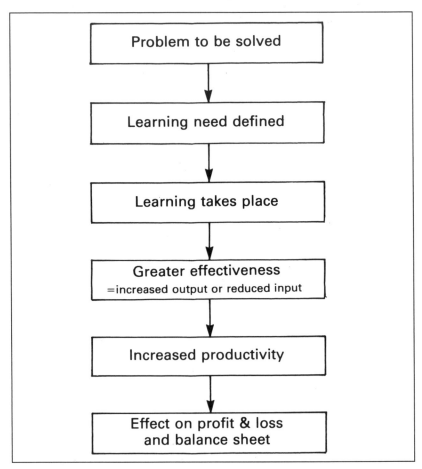

Costs and benefits from learning programmes

Organisations typically measure training *costs* as:

- the costs of dedicated staff and facilities
- the cost of courses that people are sent on.

Sometimes the salary costs of people while on courses are included. This is an opportunity cost, and should be a minimum measure of the value added while 'working'.

Typical returns might be:

- increased commercial value of individuals or teams in the market-place
- increased substitution cost of their contribution with external resource for the same skills and quality
- increased capability to satisfy customers
- increased capability to lead or motivate employees/teams to better results
- increased flexibility in the range of roles a person is able to perform
- increased opportunity for innovation through broader thinking, contacts or basic knowledge
- increased personal performance against objectives and measures of the role
- increased competitive knowledge.

It may not be easy to calculate actual figures for a particular increase in learning. However, it is often helpful to make *estimates of percentage change*. If we take productivity, then this is defined as the ratio of output to input. An improvement results from reducing inputs for the same output, or increasing output for the same input. For a major input such as time, a saving of 1 per cent is equivalent to half an hour a week; 5 per cent to two or three hours a week. The assumption is that the released time is used towards an output – revenue streams, customer satisfaction, motivating employees, or looking for further cost reduction.

The Learning Organisation encourages continuous learning in every form. Many of the significant contributors have very little marginal cost, such as time spent understanding the learning from on-the-job successes and failures, or sharing of learning and experience for the benefit of others. On the other

Figure 9.3
Capability gain

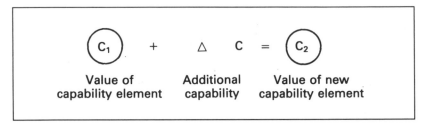

$$C_1 \quad + \quad \Delta \quad C \quad = \quad C_2$$

| Value of capability element | Additional capability | Value of new capability element |

hand, some risk-taking might turn out to be an excellent learning but very costly.

For the individual, the personal portfolio of capability (in knowledge, skills, attitudes and experience) increases, and the equation is simple, as shown in Figure 9.3.

If the 'earnings contribution' of the individual has increased as a result of the learning, then their value as an asset has increased also. This is true eg of consultancies.

The concept of added value

'Added value' is a useful accounting term for our purposes. It is defined for an enterprise as *the wealth created through the efforts of the enterprise and its people.*

It is normally calculated by the difference between the revenue streams and the costs of bought-in materials and services. It is used to pay employees, taxes, interest and depreciation. Quinn in *Intelligent Enterprise* quotes statistical data from the USA indicating that the added value from the manufacturing sector is about the same as the private services sector, at about $40,000 per head. The more profit-and-loss summaries can be devolved to smaller units the closer we can come to assessing the added value of teams within the organisation. For service providers, the price that a customer is prepared to pay for an individual or a team, less the (usually low) costs associated with providing the service, gives a figure for added value that can be taken down even to individual contributors. For overhead employees, a measure of their value is what the organisation would have to pay to an outside provider. However, it should be financially higher than this, because of the value of 'inside knowledge' – of knowing what can be realistically achieved within the culture.

This is tested in harsh commercial reality with the trend for outsourcing managed services and competitive tendering of public services. The further one goes from the 'sharp end' the less easy it is to evaluate the added value of an individual. A senior manager may make a decision one day that has a very large impact, but for considerable periods he may be just supporting and developing the added value from others.

Added value should increase as an individual becomes more mature. In the early years, investment in learning may be for a long-term return. This is true for graduate trainee programmes and apprenticeships, for example. ICL has a 'Eurograduate' training programme, hiring graduates from various European countries and training them together. Much of the 10 months' training takes the form of work assignments, but is essentially a vehicle for learning. The real investment is to create a group of cross-national friends who, in 10 years' time, will use their network and cross-cultural experiences in leadership roles.

However, added value should not be seen just in terms of money. The 'balanced score-card' approach should give each organisation a set of parameters that all have performance measures and goals. This gives customer and employee satisfaction as much importance as achieving a certain return on financial assets. Employee motivation, which affects the *way* people work, their productivity and innovation, also adds value even though it may not be directly costed.

Does all learning by definition add value? Some organisations have taken the view that so long as people take ownership for their learning, what they choose to spend their time learning is less important. Thus Rover Learning Business in the UK give a sum of money to each employee to spend *as they wish* on some knowledge or skill – the principle being that it encourages the *learning habit*. The difficulty here is to quantify the benefits. Time spent on individual learning should increase a person's contribution, either now or at some future time. That is, their added value increases. If everyone in the organisation is working at increasing their added value, the organisation will grow in value as a whole, and this must provide competitive advantage.

Eric Flamholtz, a strong proponent of human asset accounting, asserts that the aim of human resource management is to optimise human resource value. He is one of the world's experts in the difficult area of human resource accounting. He derives a complex model for the measurement of individual value. An individual's *conditional value* is the present worth of the *potential* services that could be rendered if the individual stays with the organisation for x years. The conditional value is a combination of productivity (performance), transferability (flexible skills) and promotability. The latter two are heavily influenced by the first element. This needs to be multiplied by a probability factor that he or she will stay for x years. This gives the *expected realisable value*, which is a measure of the person's value. One way to calculate the effect from a learning programme would be to estimate the change in value resulting from the change in productivity, transferability or promotability.

Few will have the patience to do this rigorously, but from time to time it may help to understand the value of investing in people to do so. Flamholtz quotes the example of the increase in individual value of attendees at a particular management development programme – where the value of those who attended against those who had not rose from $81K to $93.5K (a 15 per cent increase). The cost of the programme is not stated, but probably it was about $3,000. Such calculations are loaded with assumptions, but the important question is *does this proposed investment in our human assets give an acceptable rate of return*? Many training programmes do not because they do not address defined learning needs of the individual or the group attending.

We would like to see investments in learning capability measured and championed by organisations as much as their investment in R&D or capital assets.

POWERPOINT

Does the accounting system measure the added value of people and teams?

Are attempts made to estimate the investment return from learning activities?

The cost of learning curves

An organisation is a network of learning curves. Both individuals and groups are either on natural or programmed curves; the latter term is normally used for *planned* changes in role, or role holder, or in organisation structure. We have noted above that the learning curve of young entrants is very long; of newly promoted senior executives the expectation is often that it will be almost negligible. Every change causes loss of momentum and productivity, something that is often not taken into account when the changes are planned. This applies when individuals change jobs, new teams are formed, new subsidiaries are created, or mergers and acquisitions take place. If we look broadly at output versus cost, the graph goes like the one in Figure 9.4.

We could argue the shaded area represents the loss in effectiveness that could be avoided if we took a disciplined approach to the new learning that is needed. In turbulent fast-changing organisations this is a very significant problem. In ICL we studied the business success of country operations against the stability of their management teams, and found an unmistakeable positive correlation, even though those teams did not necessarily have 'world-class people' in them. The Learning Organisation pays a lot of attention to this, because

Figure 9.4
Output v cost

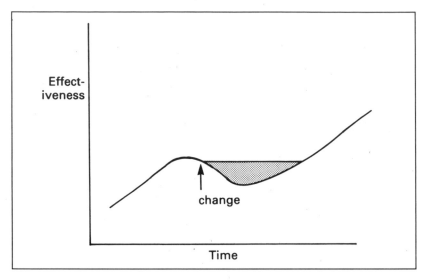

the cumulated potential costs are enormous. It will take specific and systematic action to minimise these losses.

 **POWERPOINT**

In planning organisation change, are the learning needs of the new team built in systematically in a way that takes advantage of the knowledge and experience already available in your organisation?

Pointers for action

It is a pity that no satisfactory formal way has been found for accounting for human assets. There is no doubt that the human resources in an organisation represent *the* major asset and the greatest source of growth and return. Their continued learning

– given opportunities to harness the learning – represents added asset value. However, without this they risk becoming liabilities.

Not all learning activities have a return for the organisation, but well-chosen ones always will. They should increase the capability of individuals to add value according to their skills and profession.

We believe organisations should consider the following actions:

- studying hidden costs and lost revenues that arise from 'learning deficiencies', and making a regular report or reminder of these to business units.
- evaluating added value of teams, and even individuals wherever possible, and how learning increases it
- making 'induction' – the transfer of knowledge and experience to new job incumbents and teams – a rigorous discipline in the organisation
- always to look at the costs and benefits of formal learning proposals *against* other options, such as job-based learning.

The financial effects of learning are significant, as they are of non-learning. No organisation can *afford* to give this area less than the level of attention it deserves.

10

Realising the Power of the Learning Organisation

Setting out on the journey

We hope that our description of a Learning Organisation is one that excites you and encourages you to equip yourself for the journey towards it. We recognise that every organisation has a different history, a unique culture, different goals, and therefore a different starting-point. The priority areas for action will differ from one organisation to the next.

We do hope that every reader will share in the *conviction* that increasing the learning capability of their organisation is a critical need. Having indicated a few practical areas for action at the end of each chapter, we would now like to offer a framework of change and support overall.

Managing culture change

The journey towards an effective Learning Organisation is a long one, and movement is not always consistently forwards. As ever, programmes of change require direction. Managing culture change effectively requires all the essential elements of any change management programme. We find a helpful model in this area (there are many) to be that of three interlocking circles (see Figure 10.1).

In the first circle is 'top management vision and determination'. In this context the top management team of your organisation needs to have internalised the imperative that *the rate of organisational learning must be greater than the rate of change*. They also must have a vision of what their Learning Organisation will look like in practice. However, like Richard Branson at Virgin Atlantic, who never uses the term 'empower-

Figure 10.1
Managing culture change

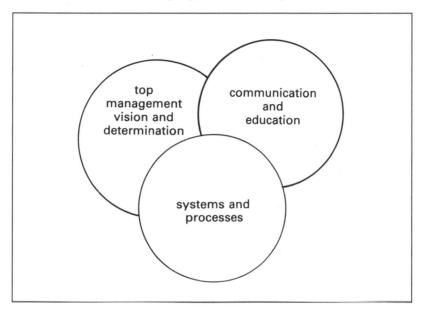

ment' yet is a role-model leader of an empowered organisation, they may well call it something else! C. K. Prahalad and Yves Doz write in *The Multinational Mission*:

> Strategic capability . . . is the inherent capacity of the organization to continuously learn about its environment, develop appropriate responses (strategies), and mobilize its resources to compete.

Your top management team may well identify better with the term 'strategic capability' than the term 'Learning Organisation' – in our view the two may be synonomous and we do recommend that the importance of learning be explicitly on the team's agenda.

In the second circle is 'communication and education'. A vision has to be communicated. This may be in a company-wide publication, but it has to be supported with a variety of communication processes. These certainly should include leaders talking through the vision with groups of people and in the various speeches they might make. Most importantly, the reasons for having this particular vision must be understood by everyone involved *for themselves*. People need to go through a 'double loop learning experience' (as Argyris would call it) to question why change is needed, and synthesise together the nature of it. The Learning Organisation as we have described it requires new ways of thinking at the level of the individual, the team and the organisation itself.

'Systems and processes', the third circle, must be adjusted at the same time. These are the 'enablers' of the supportive learning culture, and if not changed in line with the vision they will in effect become 'blockers'. These define how the organisation actually functions and which behaviours are effectively rewarded.

Understanding where you are on the journey

One cannot say an organisation is or is not in *absolute* terms a Learning Organisation. It is more or less advanced along a continuum. If it consists of more than one unit, each unit will be at different stages. Reorganisations, restructuring, mergers and alliances, new appointments, loss of key players – all these can lead to steps backwards or sideways on the journey. The question is: *how can you determine where you are, and whether you are making progress*?

We believe organisations of all sizes may see benefit in benchmarking themselves against a model of a Learning Organisation. Such a model is discussed in the Appendix as a synthesis of the areas we have been discussing in previous chapters. A method of scoring is outlined that enables each area to be assigned a suggested number of points to reflect different degrees of importance, with a potential maximum score of 1,000.

The result is the *Learning Organisation Index*.

This can be used to benchmark internally and externally, as well as track progress. It also gives clear indicators of the areas of action needed and goals to be set.

This may sound rather mechanical and contrary to the spirit of continuous learning for an organisation and the people who compose it. However, we believe that in order to turn many of the ideals and exhortations on Learning Organisations into practical reality, a businesslike approach with clear measures to track progress is essential.

Practical steps

Cultural change is normally evolutionary, as it takes time for new ways of doing things to embed themselves. Thus an objective to 'create a Learning Organisation by a certain date' is an unrealistic objective – and, as we have already pointed out, it is a journey rather than a destination. It is nevertheless helpful to know your starting–point and to have a vision of where you would like to head. These seven action steps may be helpful:

- Work with your top management team to develop a shared vision of the kind of Learning Organisation they would like to see, and ensure that they are committed to that vision so that it is built into policy, values and strategies.
- Appoint a 'champion' to lead 'the journey' who is a well-respected individual and will be taken seriously. Also identify change agents who can be catalysts in different parts of your organisation and can feed back to the champion on progress.
- Assess where your organisation stands against the Power-points we have offered.
- As a result of gaps between where you are and where you want to be, define and agree the *next few* action steps in each major area that will take you forward.

- Identify an owner for each action step.
- Encourage each owner to identify the major blockers and enablers to implementing each action step and focus attention on removing the blockers.
- Reassess where you stand every few months, and reset new action steps in each area.

A centre of excellence in learning?

Most large organisations have had training departments, sometimes linked to the personnel function, as part of their infrastructure. Some have looked at the opportunities for *outsourcing* such resources. Decisions about this should be based on what constitutes a core competence that is competitively vital for the organisation. Many standard training programmes are not in this category. We believe that the *direction* of continuous learning is unique to the culture of every organisation and needs to be an integral part of that culture.

We have mentioned elsewhere the need for *champions* and *executive co-ordination*. But in addition it helps to have people who can work with each unit to help them with learning processes – at the personal, team and organisational levels. These 'learning consultants' have a very different profile from the traditional trainer. They are skilled consultants and facilitators, able to understand the objectives and needs of either the total organisation or its units, and to respond to these with appropriate learning solutions.

The contribution lies not just in meeting the needs 'bottom-up'. Much of the enabling culture needs to be created from the perspective of the whole organisation. Thus the 'learning department' is an agent of change on behalf of the senior team. They work with:

- the definition of the type of Learning Organisation that is needed

- promoting the understanding of how to make it a practical reality
- the creation and communication of values
- the establishment of a supportive language
- the design and management of collective learning events
- the specification of IT support systems.

In smaller organisations the leadership of change and transition may not require this degree of support, but external help may be needed for specific projects.

Beyond your own organisation

Learning as a key to competitiveness is beginning to be recognised by governments, who have an obvious interest in the success of their national commerce and industry. In the UK, for example, the 'Investors in People Award' was put in place in 1992 to promote standards and better practice in training and development. 'Investors in People' has established four groups of criteria:

- *commitment* – '. . . a public commitment from the top to develop all employees to achieve its business objectives'
- *planning* – '. . . regularly reviews the training and development of all employees'
- *action* – '. . . takes action to develop individuals on recruitment and throughout their employment'
- *evaluation* – '. . . evaluates the investment in training and development, assesses achievement and how to improve future effectiveness'.

A number of 'indicators of success' are outlined against each of these groups. External assessors evaluate each of the indicators, and once the award is granted, reassessment every three years is necessary to retain it. Winning the Investors in

People Award or its equivalent in other countries can be a major benefit for your organisation – both in terms of the learning from the assessment process itself and the positive image it establishes for your organisation in the market-place.

At an individual level, competency frameworks for individuals are also receiving attention as a support for learning. In the UK, National Vocational Qualifications (NVQs) for different professions are gaining acceptance, with competency standards established from Levels 1 to 5. This type of country-wide framework enables individuals to demonstrate their knowledge and skill levels to different employers using a common standard. NVQs are particularly interesting in that they are experience related: credits are given for evidence of prior learning. This is an interesting shift from a focus on academic degrees which are based on course work rather than experience. Helping the employees in your organisation to obtain NVQ qualifications is another contribution to enhancing their employability.

Finally, those Learning Organisations that are more advanced can contribute to the common cause. They can join and participate in research bodies set up to further learning of all kinds. Information concerning such collaborations can be obtained from the European Foundation for Management Development, Rue Washington 40, BRUSSELS B-1050, tel +32 2 648 0385.

Dilemmas and paradoxes

There is no doubt that contrary forces exist in many of the areas that we have discussed. The short-term pressures that many organisations experience operate powerfully against investments for the long term. Yet it is that investment that will yield sustainable success in the future. People in very different kinds of organisations – large and small, national and international, private and public, manufacturing and service –

struggle with a range of dilemmas. Balancing them is not easy. For example:

Downsize	and Motivate people
Empower devolved units	and Maintain common values
Reduce infrastructure	and Provide corporate synergy
Encourage personal career ownership	and Develop our prime assets
Have a clear direction	and Adapt to circumstances
Lead	and Manage
Create job space	and Focus on core tasks
Build for the long term	and Meet the short-term targets
Work with fewer resources	and Take time for learning
Utilise roles for learning	and Get results as fast as possible
Expect full commitment	and Offer no job security

The need to balance these dilemmas can slow the progress of a Learning Organisation. When times are difficult and pressurised, managers fall back on the techniques and tools that have served them well in the past. The training budget will still at times be sacrificed when cost pressures hit; the Not-Invented-Here attitude will still lead to wasteful reinvention of the wheel; time for learning will not always be top priority. We need to accept and anticipate that it will not all be smooth sailing.

It is nonetheless our conviction that the Learning Organisation principles and characteristics that we have explored with you will help people in organisations to work through these apparent paradoxes. We confidently expect a clear correlation between a high 'Learning Organisation Index' and achievement of organisational success. To all those who are determined to embark on this journey, or have already done so, we wish you well.

Appendix

The Complete Learning Organisation Benchmark

Introduction

We live in a world where the pace of change is accelerating dramatically. Within organisations, adaptability is the key to success and continuous learning is the key to adaptability. Therefore one can expect a significant return on investments made to create a Learning Organisation.

The challenge is to determine where best to focus the investment of time, money and effort, when all of these are scarce. Each organisation is at a unique starting-point, with different histories, cultures and people – and facing different business issues. This appendix is intended to help you diagnose where you could most usefully take action on your journey as a Learning Organisation to achieve maximum impact.

The Complete Learning Organisation Model

The model is based on the various chapters of our book, and it brings together the 'Powerpoints' as a set of key action areas that are important practical components of the Learning Organisation. These are clustered as follows:

How to use the questionnaire

By putting relative weightings on the components of the Complete Learning Organisation Model and then answering the questions that follow, you will be able to identify:

The Complete Learning Organisation

Policy and Strategy ☐

Leadership ☐

People Management Processes ☐

Information Technology ☐

A Supportive Culture and Learning Climate ☐

Personal Learning ☐

Team Learning and Networks ☐

Organisational Learning ☐

Creating Value ☐

Enablers - - - - - - - - -▶ Environment - - - - -▶ Learning - - - - - - -▶ Value

- which components are most important to *your* organisation in creating an environment of continuous learning
- where you have the greatest gaps between the ideal and current reality
- which actions would therefore have the greatest impact in moving you towards your ideal.

The questionnaire also gives you a tool for benchmarking different parts of your organisation both internally and externally.

Step One: Weighting the Model

As a first step, take the Complete Learning Organisation Model (see previous page) and assign 1,000 points across the different components, reflecting what you believe to be the relative importance of the different components to your organisation. Two questions which may help you to attribute these weightings are:

- How crucial is this component to moving our organisation towards the ideal?
- What do we believe would be our relative competitive advantage if we excelled in this particular area?

Enter your relative weightings in the boxes of the model above. When you have completed this step, the total number of points for the complete model should add up to 1,000.

Step Two: Scoring the Powerpoints

Against each Powerpoint the following evaluation should be made for the organisation that you wish to benchmark (on a continuous scale):

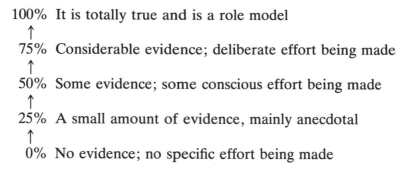

100% It is totally true and is a role model
 ↑
 75% Considerable evidence; deliberate effort being made
 ↑
 50% Some evidence; some conscious effort being made
 ↑
 25% A small amount of evidence, mainly anecdotal
 ↑
  0% No evidence; no specific effort being made

You will then have a percentage score for each question. As the questions are grouped according to the components of the Model, you should average the percentages for all the questions in one section to determine a section average. The section average should then be applied to the total number of points which you assigned to that component of the model.

When you have completed this for the nine different sections, you can then add up the points from each box to determine your

Learning Organisation Index (see page 262)

This index can be used to benchmark internally and externally, as well as track progress. Six-monthly intervals would be appropriate for measuring progress.

To determine priority target areas for action, identify the components where the gap between your actual and your ideal points is greatest. You can then review the responses to the individual questions within that section and identify those with the lowest percentage scores.

The Powerpoints have been written for an organisation. Individual leaders, human resource specialists or teams may however find it useful to adapt the 'Powerpoint questions' to apply to themselves.

1. Policy and Strategy

1.1 Defining the Learning Organisation you want to achieve

% score

Does your organisation have a template describing the characteristics of the kind of Learning Organisation it would like to be?	
Does your organisation have a framework and plan for practical implementation to achieve the desired state?	

1.2 Creating advantage for the customers

Does your organisation compare with the best competitors in innovation for customer benefit?	
Does your organisation regularly survey customer perceptions of responsiveness to their needs?	
Where feasible, does your organisation encourage partnerships with customers for mutual learning?	

1.3 Creating advantage for the employees

Do employees respond positively through opinion surveys or other methods of upward feedback about their perceptions of learning processes and how they help them?	
Would your organisation be regarded as a 'preferred employer'?	
When people voluntarily leave the organisation is it rare to give reasons such as lack of growth opportunities?	

1.4 Creating advantage for the shareholders   % score

Is your organisation structured in a way that encourages freedom and risk-taking, and minimises low added-value layers of management?	
Can your organisation show continuous productivity improvement for all its groups of employees?	
Does your organisation look for and quantify costs arising from unnecessary duplication and overlap?	
Are the skills and capabilities of your people such that they are sought after by other organisations?	

1.5 Understanding core competence

Has your organisation evaluated systematically its core competencies and are they used in strategic planning?	
Does your organisation evaluate all strategic plans in terms of its human capability to deliver?	

1.6 Clear policies

Does your organisation have a defined policy statement that specifically supports the development of a Learning Organisation?	
Does it communicate clearly to all employees the ways in which it will encourage and enhance such development?	

*Average % score for **policy and strategy**:* ☐

Multiplied by ☐ *points to give **score** of:* ☐

2. Leadership

2.1 Leadership development

% score

Does your organisation provide the opportunity to develop leadership skills to anyone with a requirement for those skills, regardless of hierarchical position?	

2.2 Visioning

Do leaders in your organisation have a clear and shared vision of where the organisation is heading?	
Is their vision developed over time with the input of many members of the organisation, at all levels?	
Is their vision communicated effectively to all within their sphere of influence, using two-way communication processes?	

2.3 Risk-taking

Do your leaders take calculated risks?	
Do they learn from mistakes and share that learning with others?	
Do they encourage creative dialogue and the putting forward of innovative, risky ideas?	
Do they encourage experimentation?	

2.4 Learning

% score

Do leaders in your organisation set the example by consistently reviewing and sharing learning points from different experiences?	
Do they welcome challenges to the status quo?	
Do leaders in your organisation each have a personal development plan?	

2.5 Empowering

Do leaders in your organisation set a clear direction within which people have freedom to determine how best to achieve?	
Do leaders only take on tasks that cannot be addressed at levels closer to the customer?	
Do they encourage independence of action and actively discourage dependent behaviour?	
Do they trust people to be competent and assume they will always do their best?	

2.6 Coaching

Do leaders within your organisation invest significant time in coaching others?	
Do they ask for coaching themselves?	

2.7 Collaborating   % score

Do leaders in your organisation collaborate effectively with their peers?	
Do they look for win-win relationships rather than win-lose?	
Are they skilled at managing alliances and joint ventures?	
Do they invest time in external and internal networking in order to build contacts and learn from others?	

2.7 Measures of performance

Are your organisation's leaders measured on both qualitative and quantitative business measures?	

2.8 Promotion criteria

Do the people who are promoted into leadership roles clearly demonstrate the characteristics of the Learning Organisation leader?
Have you established a management development framework that focuses on increasing personal value and is clearly understood by everyone?
Do the top leaders in your organisation recognise the need for a new profile of leadership qualities to be articulated and supported?

% score

Does the organisation invest in a planned, specific way in the leadership development of high-potential individuals?	
Are people recruited from outside into selected roles to bring new perspectives to the organisation?	

*Average % score for **leadership**:* ☐

Multiplied by ☐ *points to give **score** of:* ☐

3. People Management Processes

3.1 Performance evaluation and feedback

Is the process for evaluating and discussing performance one that encourages the input of data from all relevant sources to help with personal development?	
Do the majority of managers and staff feel that the culture supports **open** feedback?	
Is the primary ownership of feedback with the individual?	
Is there a flexibility of choice in the approach to performance feedback, depending on individual preference and readiness?	

3.2 Learning plans   % score

Do individuals at all levels have a learning plan that they personally own, covering knowledge, skills, attitudes, and experience?	
Do such plans specify learning objectives and utilise a range of learning solutions to achieve them?	
Are they both reviewed and renewed regularly?	

3.3 Describing roles

Do all roles in the organisation have a set of specified accountabilities rather than series of tasks?	
Does each role have a profile of knowledge, skills, attitudes and experience appropriate to it, split clearly into entry criteria and learning opportunities?	

3.4 Selection

Is a key aspect of selection for posts the matching of the core entry criteria with the experience requirements from individual learning plans?	

3.5 Induction

Do new recruits and job changers have professional, individualised induction programmes that work from their learning needs?	
Is the same done where feasible for new teams?	

3.6 Resource management
% score

Do you have a clear definition of the skills and roles that should be core resources in order to give your organisation unique competitive advantage?	
Do you have partnership resources that identify and share in your organisation's success?	
Do you help your part-time resources with their own continual learning?	
Does your organisation have a continuing strategy for acquiring new people, both in terms of fresh young people, and through deliberate infeed of new ideas at all levels?	

3.7 Career management

Does your organisation have 'role families' which outline the core entry knowledge, skills, attitudes and experience requirements for stages of increased value?	
Are they accessible to individuals for the purpose of their own career planning?	
Are the systems used for succession planning and potential rating appropriate for the Learning Organisation you would like to have?	

3.8 Rewards

Does your organisation have a remuneration system that rewards continuous learning and its application, rather than fixed jobs?	
Does it have a clear view of what should be rewarded by base pay and what by variable bonus?	

3.9 Non-monetary rewards   % score

Does your organisation have award schemes recognising learning achievements that are valued by recipients and respected by colleagues?	
Does your organisation have awards for innovation that are prestigious and valued?	
Does your organisation use special learning experiences as part of the reward portfolio?	

3.10 Opinion surveys

Does your organisation utilise regular surveys of employee opinion that enable it to track cultural changes?	
Does the survey include questions that support specific changes designed to achieve a better Learning Organisation?	

3.11 Skills planning

Does every part of your organisation have suitable diagnostic tools to match capabilities with business demands?	
Does your organisation have a strategic planning process that recognises and defines the necessary human resource capabilities for success?	
Is there a systematic process for skills planning that derives from the business plan down to team and individual learning plans?	
Do the needs for investment in skills get built into the final business plan?	

3.12 General processes   % score

Looking at all the key processes in your organisation which affect people: – do they encourage rather than punish experimentation and risk-taking?	
– do they put decision-taking as close to the point of impact of each decision as possible?	
– do they trust people to use the organisation's resources sensibly?	
– do they encourage sharing rather than reinforce tribal boundaries?	

*Average % score for **people management processes**:* ☐

Multiplied by ☐ *points to give **score** of:* ☐

4. The Use of Information Technology

4.1 Using groupware

Does your organisation encourage its teams to exploit groupware applications for more effective interworking?	
Has your organisation exploited information technology to support the sharing of knowledge across boundaries?	

4.2 Organisational memories

Do you have a means of capturing knowledge into databases accessible to everyone in your organisation?	

4.3 Skills databases   % score

Does your organisation hold a skills database?	
Does your skills database enable you to list learning/ development needs as well as skills acquired?	
Is it used regularly to bring temporary teams together to address customer requirements?	
Does it enable you to assemble teams of people from different parts of the organisation?	

4.4 Information availability and access

Do you provide the infrastructure for and encourage the use of electronic bulletin boards to facilitate knowledge-sharing across your organisation?	
Do you take information-sharing seriously enough to invest in a senior person or team accountable for making it happen?	

4.5 Technology for learning

Do you use multimedia and other technology-based training approaches for your organisation, where they are the cost-effective solution?	
Do you have learning resource centres available to people in your organisation?	

4.6 Exploring options

Do you make available software-based Learning Option Guides and/or Career Option Guides for individuals in your organisation, to enable them to plan their own learning and development?	

4.7 Understanding customers   % score

Do you exploit information technology in helping you learn about your customers' requirements?	

4.8 Information for everybody

Do your employees have the information they need at any given time to make business decisions and track key performance measures?	

4.9 Information security

Have you ensured that you have the right levels of security for your IT data?	

4.10 Information standards

Have you established and communicated standards for the input to your information networks and knowledge databases?	

4.11 Information control

Do you have processes in place that direct information to the people who need it without creating 'information overload'?	

*Average % score for **use of information technology**:* [   ]

Multiplied by [   ] *points to give **score** of:* [   ]

5. A Supportive Culture

5.1 *Learning explicitly supported*   % score

Does the organisation have a defined and communicated approach to learning?	
Is the culture in your organisation one that explicitly or implicitly supports a **range** of learning behaviours?	

5.2 *Value sets*

Does the organisation have a set of values which includes: – a commitment to continuous learning for individuals and teams?	
– the sharing of knowledge and experience in the organisation for the benefit of all?	
– the desire to be a competitive Learning Organisation?	

5.3 *A language of learning*

Is there a common language about capability that meets the needs of your organisation, and is used throughout the relevant people-management processes?	
Is the term 'Learning' in common currency, and is it used in such a way that good learning practices are supported?	

5.4 What the top people say and do   % score

When times are hard or 'end-of-year' financial pressures are heavy, is the budget for learning still protected?	
Do senior leaders show concern for the level of spending and resourcing for learning in relation to competition?	
Do senior leaders actively push the specialists in the organisation to explore new ways of learning?	
Do senior leaders look for opportunities to mention the importance of continuous shared learning in speeches, inspirational letters, company newsletters and other forms of communication?	
Do senior leaders build items relating to learning achievements into objective-setting and reward schemes?	

5.5 'OK' behaviours

Does your organisation have a shared understanding of the behaviours that are, and those that are not, supportive of a continuous learning climate?	
Does it use this to check from time to time whether people in the organisation believe such behaviours are supported in reality?	
Are behaviours which are clearly against the agreed set discussed with the individual concerned?	

5.6 Time and money

Does your organisation encourage people to invest time in continuous and job-related learning activities?	

% score

Is there a defined learning budget, owned at the lowest level in the organisation?	
Is the learning budget regarded as a key investment and non-tradeable?	

5.7 Ownership of learning

Is it clear to all individuals that they need personally to own their learning?	
Do the supporting processes emphasise and empower such ownership?	
Is there an organisational champion and programme leader of Learning Organisation principles?	

5.8 Sharing knowledge and experience

Does your organisation have a 'knowledge management' team, with a respected and effective director?	
Does every individual know that he or she is expected to access a library of data and experiences owned by the organisation?	
Is a process established throughout your organisation for people to share their learning through contributing to an appropriate library or database?	

*Average % score for **culture**:* ☐

Multiplied by ☐ *points to give **score** of:* ☐

6. Personal Learning

6.1 Encouraging employability   % score

Is the concept of increasing people's employability openly discussed in your organisation?	
Is one of your organisational objectives to offer challenges and opportunities to increase people's long-term employability?	

6.2 Understanding learning styles

Does your organisation offer people the facility to assess their own learning styles?	
Does your organisation cater for different learning styles in the development opportunities that it provides?	

6.3 From training to learning

Does your organisation focus on learning and its link to performance rather than simply training?	

6.4 Ranges of learning options

Are people in your organisation aware of and using a range of development options?	
Are managers in your organisation encouraging a wide range of approaches to people development?	
Does your organisation support them with some form of Learning Options Guide?	

6.5 Incidental learning   % score

Is taking time to reflect on lessons learned acceptable and encouraged within your organisational culture?	
Are lessons learned shared with others?	
Are people in your organisation encouraged to question the status quo?	
Do changes take place as a result of this questioning?	

6.6 Learning from life

Is the learning available from non-work activities taken into account in recruitment decisions?	
Are people in your organisation encouraged to get involved in activities outside the workplace?	
Are these activities recognised and dicussed within the work organisation?	

6.7 Action learning

Does your organisation use action learning to develop individuals and the business?	

6.8 Self-managed learning

% score

Does your organisation have processes to support self-managed learning?	
Is there a shared understanding of business direction within which people can develop their skills?	
Are your senior managers/leaders role models for self-managed learning?	

6.9 Coaching by all

Does everyone in your organisation consider coaching to be an integral part of their role?	
Does your organisation reward coaching behaviour?	
Are a range of people – including line managers – from around the organisation contributing to training/learning events?	
Are there many networks or special interest groups who meet to learn from each other?	

6.10 Questioning and unlearning

Are people in your organisation prepared to change or eliminate 'sacred cows' – things that are deeply embedded in the organisation as a result of history?	

*Average % score for **effectiveness of personal learning**:*

Multiplied by _____ *points to give **score** of:*

7. Team Learning

7.1 Using teams   % score

Does your organisation recognise the value of teamwork explicitly: for example, are quality improvement awards or other visible recognition mechanisms awarded to teams as well as individuals?	
Does your objective-setting process include the possibility of setting team objectives, not just individual objectives?	
Do your criteria for promotion include the teamworking skills of individuals?	

7.2 Using teams for learning

Are the opportunities for learning among the considerations taken into account when teams are composed?	

7.3 Learning together

Do teams in your organisation take time to review learning points from the experiences they have as a group?	
Are these learning points captured in some way and shared with others?	

7.4 Team effectiveness

Is facilitation support available to teams in reviewing the effectiveness of their processes?	

7.5 Boundary-spanning teams   % score

Does your organisation invest in developing cross-cultural sensitivity and related skills to support 'boundary-less' teams?	
Do you involve external people – customers, suppliers, perhaps competitors – in your internal activities?	
Do people involved in direct teamwork with people from outside bring the things they learn from them into the organisation?	

7.6 Supporting networks

Does your organisation support and encourage informal networks?	
Is there a mechanism for capturing and sharing the information and knowledge built up by such networks?	

7.7 Work communities – people with common interests

Are work communities recognised as having added value for the individuals within them?	
Is contact between members of a work community facilitated or encouraged?	
Are their development needs as a work community considered?	

*Average % score for **effectiveness of team learning**:* ☐

Multiplied by ☐ *points to give **score** of:* ☐

8. Organisational Learning

8.1 Organisational structures   % score

Is your organisational structure focused on maximising client responsiveness, innovation and learning?	
Does it encourage teamwork and discourage functional and tribal boundaries wherever possible?	
Are supporting functions primarily providing services, sharing information and adding value?	
Where there are boundaries in the structure, are they transparent, and are there mechanisms for dialogue (both formal and informal) to take place across them?	

8.2 Sharing best practice

Does your organisation have, for each customer-centred process, ways of collating and distributing information, collected at all levels, and for its collective interpretation?	
Does your organisation have a variety of mechanisms for sharing best practice in every area of the organisation's activities?	
Is it normal in your organisation for younger people to have personal mentors and guides to help them with their learning about the organisation, how it functions, and how to achieve their goals?	

8.3 Benchmarking   % score

Is there a systematic benchmarking methodology operated consistently throughout your organisation?	
Does it include internal, competitive, functional and process benchmarks?	
Is there senior sponsorship and programme management?	
Is it built into the expectations of every department, team and individual that learning from benchmarking is a **normal** way of life, and are achievement targets regularly reset as a result?	
Are there specific benchmarks relating to learning?	

8.4 Learning from mergers and acquisitions

Does your organisation have a check-list for 'due diligence' to be made in cases of mergers, acquisitions or alliances, which enables assessment of the proposed partner against the characteristics of a Learning Organisation?	
Does your organisation have a systematic approach to respecting **and** absorbing/disseminating the accumulated learning of the new partner?	
Would your organisation be prepared to reorient its strategy, structure, systems and culture as a result of the new partnership?	

8.5 External scanning   % score

Does your organisation have a credible process for examining the external trends that affect its business?	
Is there a mechanism for sharing such findings amongst key influencers and learning together about the implications for change?	
Is strategic planning carried out as a shared learning experience?	

8.6 Collective learning

Does your organisation ensure that regular 'educational' events take place for appropriate groups across the organisation's internal boundaries?	
Does your organisation look for opportunities for collective problem-solving?	
Does your organisation hold events for learning new capabilities together?	

*Average % score for **effectiveness of organisational learning**:* ☐

Multiplied by ☐ *points to give **score** of:* ☐

9. Valuing Learning

9.1 Learning and the profit & loss account

Does your organisation link revenue plans to the capability that is needed to achieve them?	
Does your organisation examine lost revenues and relate them to lack of knowledge, skills, attitudes or experience in individuals, **or** to ineffective organisational use of those?	

% score

Can your organisation assess and talk about costs arising from aspects of ineffectiveness as a Learning Organisation?	
Does your organisation look for and quantify costs arising from unnecessary duplication and overlap?	

9.2 Assets and liabilities

Does your organisation visibly treat people as assets and show concern that they are continually appreciating and not depreciating?	
Does your organisation periodically and systematically assess its human liabilities?	

9.3 Measuring added value from learning

Does the accounting system measure the added value of people and teams?	
Are attempts made to estimate the investment return from learning activities?	

9.4 Efficient learning curves

In planning organisation change, are the learning needs of the new team built in systematically in a way that takes advantage of the knowledge and experience already available in your organisation?	

*Average % score for **valuing of learning**:* ☐

Multiplied by ☐ *points to give **score** of:* ☐

LEARNING ORGANISATION INDEX

	A score	B ideal	C gap
Policy and Strategy			
Leadership			
People Management Processes			
Information Technology			
Supportive Culture			
Personal Learning			
Team Learning			
Organisational Learning			
Valuing Learning			
LEARNING ORGANISATION INDEX		1,000	

In Column A, insert the score you have calculated for each section of the questionnaire. In Column B, insert the ideal number of points out of 1,000 which you allocated across the different components of the Complete Learning Organisation Model. In Column C, enter the difference between Columns A and B. Those areas with the greatest gap in Column C are those on which you should consider placing a priority for action.

References

ARGYRIS C. *On Organisational Learning*. Cambridge MA, Blackwell, 1993

ARGYRIS C. and SCHON D. *A Theory in Practice: Increasing professional effectiveness*. San Francisco, Jossey-Bass, 1976

BAIN G. *Annual Report of the London Business School*. March 1994

BLAKELEY K. *The Learning Organisation – Achieving competitive advantage through learning*. M.Sc. Thesis, 1993

BOISOT M. *Information and Organisation – The manager as anthropologist*. London, HarperCollins, 1987

BOWER D. 'Becoming a Learning Organisation – the experience of the Rover Group'. *Learning More about Learning Organisations*, AMED Focus Paper, October 1993

BURGOYNE J. 'Creating a Learning Organisation'. *Royal Society of Arts Journal*. April 1992

BURGOYNE J., PEDLER M. and BOYDELL T. *The Learning Company – A strategy for sustainable development*. Maidenhead, McGraw-Hill, 1991

CRITCHLEY B. 'Can organisations really learn?' *Learning More about Learning Organisations*, AMED Focus Paper, October 1993

DE BONO E. *Lateral Thinking for Management*. Harmondsworth, Penguin Books, 1982

DE GEUS A. 'Planning as learning'. *Harvard Business Review*. April–May 1988

DE POTTER P. *et al*. *Technology as an Instrument for Learning Organisation Development*. European Union CCAM Contract #76246, 1994

DE PREE M. *Leadership is an Art*. New York, Doubleday, 1989

DIXON N. *The Organisational Learning Cycle*. Maidenhead. McGraw-Hill, 1994

DRUCKER P. 'The coming of the new organisation'. *Harvard Business Review*. January–February 1988.

FLAMHOLTZ E. *Human Resource Accounting*. 2nd edn. San Francisco, Jossey-Bass, 1985

FOY N. *Empowering People at Work*. Aldershot, Gower, 1994

FREEDLAND J. 'A network heaven in your own front room'. *The Guardian*. 30 April 1994

GARRATT B. *Creating a Learning Organisation*. Cambridge, Director Books, 1990

GARRATT B. *The Learning Organisation and the Need for Directors Who Think*. Aldershot, Gower, 1987

GARRATT B. *Learning to Lead*. London, HarperCollins, 1991

GIBBONS A. and GREENE M. 'Learning Logs for Self-Development'. *Training and Development*. February 1991

GILES W. J. and ROBINSON D. F. *Human Asset Accounting*. London, Institute of Personnel Management/Institute of Cost and Management Accountants, 1972

GUY R. R., HOLDEN F. and DICKINSON P. 'ICL learning about self-managed learning'. *Industrial and Commercial Training*. Vol. 26, No. 4, 1994

HANDY C. *The Age of Unreason*. London, Basic Books, 1989

HANDY C. *The Empty Raincoat*. London, Hutchinson, 1994

HANDY C. *Managing the Dream: the Learning Organisation*. Gemini Consulting Monograph, 1992

HANDY C. *Understanding Organisations*. London, Penguin, 1976

HONEY P. 'Establishing a learning regime'. *Organisations & People*. January 1994

HONEY P. and MUMFORD A. *A Manual of Learning Styles*. Maidenhead, Honey,, 1986

IDS. 'Managing upward appraisal'. *Management Pay Review*. No. 159, May 1994

KAKABADSE A. *The Politics of Management*. Aldershot, Gower, 1983

KATZENBACH J. and SMITH D. *The Wisdom of Teams*. Boston, Harvard Business School Press, 1993

KOLB D. *Experiential Learning*. Englewood Cliffs, Prentice Hall, 1984

KOTTER J. *A Force for Change: How leadership differs from management*. New York, Macmillan, 1990

LIKERT R. *The Human Organisation – Its management and value*. New York, McGraw-Hill, 1967

MAYO A. J. *Managing Careers – Strategies for organisations*. London, Institute of Personnel Management, 1991

MAYO A. J. and HADAWAY A. J. 'Cultural adaptation: the ICL–Nokia Data merger 1991–2'. *Journal of Management Development*. Vol. 13, No. 2, 1994

MCNEIL G. 'Pyramid felling'. *International Management*. October 1993

MEGGINSON D. *Planned and Emergent Learning*. Sheffield, David Megginson Associates, 1994

MILLS D. Q. and FRIESEN B. 'The Learning Organisation'. *European Management Journal*. Vol. 10, No. 2, June 1992

MINTZBERG H. *Power in and around Organisations*. New Jersey, Prentice Hall, 1983

MULLER J. and WATTS D. 'Modelling and muddling: the long route to new organisations'. *European Management Journal*. Vol. 11, September 1993

MUMFORD A. *Developing Top Managers*. Aldershot, Gower, 1988

MUMFORD A. *How Managers Can Develop Managers*. Aldershot, Gower, 1993

MUMFORD A. 'Improving the Experience of Learning'. EFMD Forum. March, 1993

NONAKA I. 'The knowledge-creating company'. *Harvard Business Review*. November–December 1991

OSTROFF F. and SMITH D. 'The horizontal organisation'. *McKinsey Quarterly*. 1992

PEARN M. A. and KANDOLA R. *Toolkit for the Learning Organisation*. Oxford, 1993

PETERS T. *Liberation Management*. New York, Knopf, 1992

PRAHALAD C. K. 'A strategy for growth: the role of core competence in the organisation.' EFMD Forum. October 1993

PRAHALAD C. K. and DOZ Y. *The Multinational Mission*. New York, Macmillan, 1987

PRAHALAD C. K. and HAMEL G. 'The core competence of the corporation'. *Harvard Business Review*. No. 3, 1990

QUINN J. B. *Intelligent Enterprise*. New York, The Free Press, 1992

REVANS R. *The Origins of Action Learning*. Bromley and Lund, Chartwell-Bratt, 1982

SADLER P. *The Management of Talent*. London, Economist Books Ltd, 1993

SATTELBERGER T. *Die Lernende Organisation*. Wiesbaden, Gabler, 1991

SCHEIN E. *Career Dynamics – Matching organisational and individual needs*. Reading MA, Addison-Wesley, 1978

SCHWARTZ P. *The Art of the Long View*. New York, Doubleday, 1991

SENGE P. *The Fifth Discipline*. New York, Doubleday, 1990

STAHL T., NYHAN B. and D'ALOJA P. *The Learning Organisation*. Brussels, Eurotecnet, 1993

SWIERINGA J. and WIERDSMA A. *Becoming a Learning Organisation*. Reading MA, Addison-Wesley, 1978

TICHY N. M. and DEVANNA M. A. *The Transformational Leader*. New York, John Wiley and Sons, 1986

VAN DEN BROECK H. 'Business trends and the Learning Organisation'. Paper presented at ECLO Conference, May 1994

Index

Other titles in the Developing Strategies series

From Leanness to Fitness: Developing corporate muscle

Michel Syrett and Jean Lammiman

Developed out of Japanese just-in-time manufacturing methods and the worldwide quality revolution, *the lean organisation* is here to stay, because it can provide the essential *fitness* required to innovate, capture fresh markets, and secure long-term success. Yet companies that ignore the people implications of leanness are all too often debilitated by relentless cost-cutting. Delayered structures can deliver a sustained competitive edge provided that constant 'health checks' keep track of stress levels, spans of control, and support mechanisms for both teams and individuals. Communications, appraisal, and development systems must empower employees and encourage them to harness their knowledge, creativity and expertise for the good of the enterprise. HR practitioners in particular have a new role to play as 'corporate psychologists', building up business muscle and slimming down where necessary while avoiding the dangers of 'anorexia'.

Michel Syrett and Jean Lammiman illuminate all these crucial tasks by drawing on the experiences of organisations ranging from BP, Rolls Royce Motor Cars and Rank Xerox to BMW and the Body Shop, revealing along the way both the benefits and the pitfalls of lean working.

1997   144 pages   Royal paperback   ISBN 0 85292 685 5   **£19.95**

Leadership for Strategic Change

Christopher Ridgeway and Brian Wallace

Effective strategic change leadership means seeing beyond day-to-day issues towards forging a new vision for the business. It means using influence to get others on board or helping them to achieve results. It also means choosing the right style – flexible, participative or more controlling – to adopt in specific circumstances.

This book enables potential change leaders to think through the issues, assess their core skills, put them into context, and proceed to action. Stimulating questionnaires test for different kinds of leadership ability. Vivid case-studies spell out lessons from organisations that have undergone major change, while frank and extended interviews with key players in change initiatives offer valuable insider comment.

1996   240 pages   Royal paperback   ISBN 0 85292 613 8   **£19.95**

Ethical Leadership

Stephen Connock
and Ted Johns

Today's managers are constantly faced with acute ethical dilemmas; many may feel under pressure to sacrifice personal beliefs to corporate gain. Yet most books on business ethics are obscure and overtheoretical. This bold new text adopts a considered but completely practical approach that has nothing to do with saintliness and everything to do with organisational effectiveness and management action. Topics covered in depth, with stimulating company examples, include:

- balancing the needs and perspectives of different stakeholders
- codes of business conduct and common ethical issues about gifts, hospitality, confidentiality and conflicts of interest
- establishing the values to promote the right behaviour
- implementing core principles
- the roles of training and HR.

1995   240 pages   Royal paperback   ISBN 0 85292 561 1   **£19.95**

The Communicating Organisation

Michael Blakstad and Aldwyn Cooper

Internal communication is not just part of PR or crisis management but a vital strategic tool. This pioneering book explains why employers need to devote more resources to this vital area. Drawing on their own consultancy experience, the authors reveal a number of fascinating case-studies, including:

- how the technology division of the **Atomic Energy Authority** carried out an in-depth audit and built its privatisation programme on the perceptions of people within, as well as outside
- how **Price Waterhouse** turned its consultancy skills on itself, forged a new philosophy, and communicated it to every employee
- how **Meridian Broadcasting** recruited its entire staff, moulded them into a single unit, and was on the air within 14 months of being granted a licence.

1995   208 pages   Royal paperback   ISBN 0 85292 575 1   **£18.95**

Empowering Change
The role of people management

Christopher Ridgeway
and Brian Wallace

New paperback edition

Successful change initiatives – when companies set out to restructure themselves, internationalise, become market leaders, or develop a high performance culture – depend crucially on quality people management.

To elaborate this central claim, leading consultants Ridgeway and Wallace draw on the experiences of directors, managers, and staff wrestling daily with change in organisations such as Reckitt and Colman, Shell International, and Allied Lyons. They explore the need for effective collaboration between the line and HR, the skills many personnel professionals urgently need to acquire, ways of identifying the 'stakeholders' in change, the inevitable casualties, and the choice between revolutionary and evolutionary methods.

Later chapters set out 'critical success factors' for effective change, and examine the key roles of managers as change leaders and of HR professionals as strategic partners. Today, continuous change – as opposed to fretful tinkering when things go wrong – is central to every strong business. This powerful book will help companies meet the challenge head-on.

'Personnel professionals who see the need to move away from their traditional administrative . . . roles to that of "change expert" or "internal consultant" . . . will find this book one of the most useful on the market.'

Henley Newslink

1995   224 pages   Royal paperback   ISBN 0 85292 627 8   **£18.95**

Managing the Mosaic
Diversity in action

Rajvinder Kandola
and Johanna Fullerton

Special Commendation winner at the 1995
Management Consultancies Association Book Awards

Today, all organisations have to confront the challenge of diverse workforces. Yet many equal opportunity initiatives, in particular target-setting and positive action, which focus on specific groups such as women or ethnic minorities, are fundamentally flawed. To be effective, diversity strategies must tap into the talents of all staff, not just those from selected groups.

In this provocative but highly practical book, Rajvinder Kandola and Johanna Fullerton – chartered occupational psychologists at the Pearn Kandola practice in Oxford – set out to separate myth from reality. Drawing on a wide-ranging literature search, extensive experience of working within companies and a survey of almost 300 organisations, they give clear evidence that group-based equal opportunity policies are divisive and seldom successful.

Effective diversity strategies, pioneered by companies such as International Distillers and Vintners, are summed up in a detailed new model and linked to the ideal of the 'learning organisation', whose essential elements are flexibility, an empowering culture, universal benefits and business-related training for whoever needs it. Demographic changes, legislation, and increasingly globalised markets mean that diversity is now of central concern for all employers. This book provides definitive solutions to their problems.

'[*Managing the Mosaic*] makes a compelling case for the better management of the resources of the business: people with their wide variety of attributes, concerns, values and needs.'
The judges' panel, 1995 MCA Book Awards

1994   200 pages   Royal paperback   ISBN 0 85292 556 5   **£18.95**

The Reality of Strategic HRM

*Michael Armstrong
and Phil Long*

This pioneering piece of research, based on in-depth interviews in organisations that have renewed themselves through getting to grips with change, sets out to separate rhetoric from reality.

The first section examines current thinking on the nature of 'strategy', 'strategic management' and 'strategic HRM'. In the real world, argue the authors, organisations do not forge fixed blueprints for years ahead but a general sense of direction to help steer them through a chaotic environment. The authors then turn to the experiences of the Rover Group, Pilkington Optronics, and other organisations from both private and public sectors, which all provided access to members of the top management team.

The first section draws out the lessons, demonstrating how personnel professionals can add value and enhance competitiveness, and how their contribution can usefully be evaluated. Although the book questions some of the more naive claims made for strategic HRM, its approach is both positive and strongly practical, making available the achievements of many leading-edge organisations as a stimulus to others.

'Practical, no-nonsense and succinct, this analysis of what makes strategic HRM a reality will appeal both to practitioners and students.'

Personnel Today

1994   224 pages   Royal paperback   ISBN 0 85292 563 8   **£19.95**

Changing Culture
New organisational approaches

Allan Williams, Paul Dobson
and Mike Walters

This invaluable book draws on the experiences of major organisations to reveal how culture change can help drive through significant improvements in performance, efficiency, and profitability. Strategic thinking is vital, but the core personnel skills – appraisal, communication, remuneration and training – also play a key role. The book explains just why culture remains crucial, and includes stimulating, up-to-date case-studies from the Royal Mail, McVitie's and James Cropper plc.

'One of the most useful recent works on corporate culture . . . a good starting-point for any manager.'

Long-Range Planning

1993   Second edition 328 pages   Royal paperback
ISBN 0 85292 533 6   **£19.95**

Management Development
Strategies for action

Alan Mumford

Professor Alan Mumford shows organisations how to combine formal and informal approaches to management development, how to compare internal and external courses, how to look far more closely at the different needs and learning styles of individuals, and how to help them learn from experience. Management development, he argues, can be improved dramatically – provided we are willing to go back to first principles and continuously improve our techniques.

'A valuable and highly detailed summary of the current state of the debate . . . a thought-provoking book, a blend of anecdotal and empirical data which avoids the pitfalls of providing "easy" answers and leaves the reader to draw his or her own conclusions.'
Tony Crompton, Industrial and Commercial Training

1993   Second edition 248 pages   Royal paperback
ISBN 0 85292 518 2   **£18.95**

Managing Careers
Strategies for organisations

Andrew Mayo

Effective career management involves a partnership between employers committed to continuous development and employees who take personal responsibility for themselves. Andrew Mayo draws on wide practical experience and a deep knowledge of the literature to explain how to create a framework appropriate to your organisational culture and adaptable to changing business needs. Today, he argues, all companies face the challenge of harmonising corporate and individual goals. This much-acclaimed book clearly demonstrates the value of a systematised approach to personal development planning.

'This is the best and most practical guide to career management I have read. Personnel people will find it an invaluable bible.'
Garth Heron, United Distillers

'A highly practical reaffirmation of the possibility of managed careers . . . and of the benefits that can follow for organisations and people.'
Peter Herriot, Personnel Management

1991   320 pages   Royal paperback   ISBN 0 85292 467 4   **£19.95**